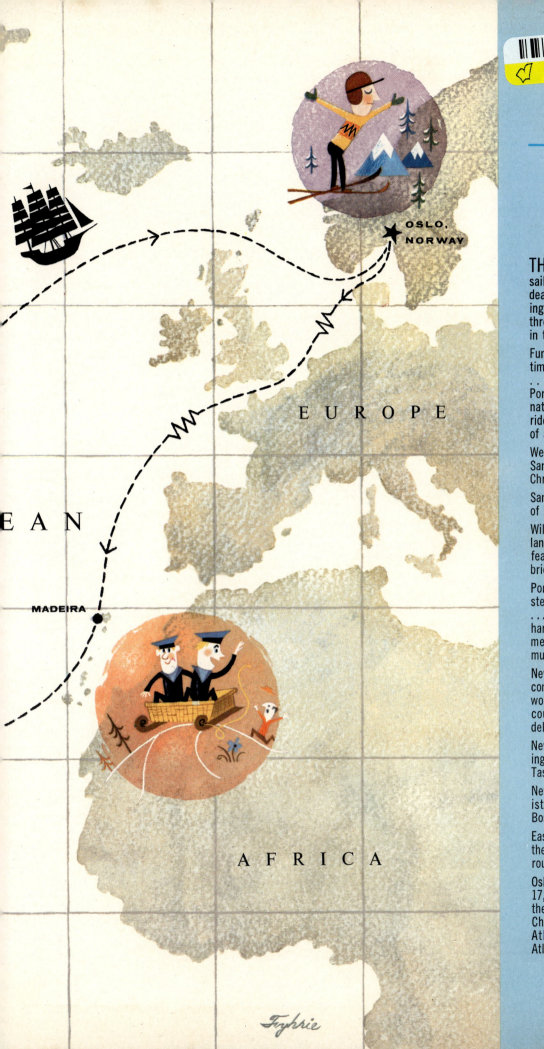

THE CHRISTIAN RADICH

sailed from Oslo, Norway, in the dead of winter. Her cadets, making their first trip to sea, sailed through the worst Atlantic storm in ten years.

Funchal, Madeira . . . landed in time for the New Year celebration . . . a sky full of fireworks . . . a Portuguese festival with colorful native music . . . and a break-neck ride down a mountain . . . the thrill of all thrills!

Westward across the Atlantic to San Juan, by the 1492 route of Christopher Columbus.

San Juan, the singing eloquence of Pablo Casals' cello!

Willemstad, Curaçao . . . old Holland in the Caribbean . . . Dutch feasts . . . dancing . . . the famous bridge of boats!

Port-of-Spain, Trinidad . . . native steel bands . . . Calypso singers . . . limbo and jump-up dances . . . harvest of the sugar cane . . . a memorable parade of haunting music and vivid color!

New York . . . photographed in a completely new technique, as only world famous "lensman" Weegee could do it. It will leave you delighted and amazed!

New England waters . . . a thrilling encounter with a U. S. Navy Task Force!

New England ashore . . . the artistry of Arthur Fiedler and the Boston Pops Orchestra!

Eastward across the Atlantic by the 1000 A.D. Northern (Viking) route of Leif Ericsson.

Oslo, a triumphant return after 17,500 miles across the waters of the Skagerrak, North Sea, English Channel, Bay of Biscay, South Atlantic, Caribbean and North Atlantic.

YOU ARE THERE IN CINEMIRACLE.

OSLO, NORWAY

EUROPE

MADEIRA

AFRICA

EAN

Fyhrie

Foreword

LOUIS DE ROCHEMONT has selected a challenging, epic subject for the first Cinemiracle presentation. A story about boys going to sea, to be trained on an old-fashioned sailing ship; perhaps not to become professional seamean, but to develop character, courage and integrity, and to prepare for careers in a difficult and bewildering world. The windjammer *Christian Radich* in her conflict with the elements provides the young cadets with every variety of difficult and challenging experience.

In this atomic and electronic age, science has demonstrated that it can accomplish miracles. The new science of electronics has been employed in the operation and perfection of the all-new Cinemiracle medium. For the first time, it will be your privilege and pleasure to go aboard a windjammer, the *Christian Radich*. On this windjammer you share a life of thrills dreamed of, but never before experienced. Through the handiwork of Louis de Rochemont and his great team of associates, this film was made possible. The millions of dollars that National Theatres, Inc., invested in research and production costs provided them with new and improved technical equipment.

This great effort on the part of scientists, producers, directors, writers, artists and technicians was made for one purpose—to entertain you. It gives you a new experience in seeing motion pictures with a scope that matches the vision of the human eye. You will watch wall-to-wall projection, and hear 7-track stereo Hi-Fi sound, resulting in a delightful experience long to be remembered.

We are most happy to play a part in the continuing development of the motion picture, thereby bringing to the theatre patron a greater measure of enjoyment.

Sincerely,

April 8, 1958
Los Angeles, California

Elmer C. Rhoden, President, National Theatres, Inc.

4

THE STORY OF

Louis de Rochemont's

WINDJAMMER

Including *The School of the Sea* and *Sailing a Square-Rigger*

by

CAPTAIN ALAN VILLIERS

Articles by

Elmer C. Rhoden · Russell H. McCullough · Sven Erik Libaek

Gayne Rescher · William H. Terry · James W. Hardiman

a modern adventure in CINEMIRACLE

PUBLISHED BY RANDOM HOUSE · NEW YORK

A father's letter to his Windjammer son

Dear Olav:

You may wonder why I sent you to sea to be trained in an old-fashioned sailing-ship, when all your schooling has been strictly modern.

I am not interested in seeing you become a sailing-ship commander, for there will never again be such ships to command. But I am interested in seeing you become a man. Your academic schooling has served its purpose. You are growing up in an atomic age when there are more likely to be spaceships than Cape Horn windjammers. Remember this: no matter what man may develop and no matter how smart he might think himself, there will never be anything more important than man himself—the full man, the man of integrity, courage, character— the man able to take his place in a bewildering world.

That's where your windjammer will help. In her conflict with the elements, in the hard knocks and the hard lessons she will throw at you daily, you will find your self, my son. It doesn't matter that you may never be a sailor. You will be a man when you return from this voyage.

Look after yourself, get along with your shipmates, be the first on deck at the call for "all hands," and when you're aloft, remember—one hand for the ship and one hand for yourself. Do these things and you'll be all right.

Love, Father

Grateful acknowledgment is made to
JAMES W. HARDIMAN who created and edited this book,
to Norman C. Bouse for art direction,
to Belle Becker Sideman for editorial consultation
and to the following photographers for their still photographs: Ormond Gigli, Finn Bergan, Aasmund Revold, Don Christie, Raul Perestrello, Fred Fischer, Sam Rosenberg, Tex Brewer.

Contents

This book was produced by Ray Freiman

The School o

By Captain Alan Villiers

Alan Villiers began his career in sailing ships when he was fifteen years old — about the age of some of the bright young cadets in WINDJAMMER. Today Mr. Villiers can look back on a life spent largely under sail, a life rich in adventure as well as in prolific literary output. Mr. Villiers' most recent voyage under sail—piloting the MAYFLOWER II from Plymouth, England, to Plymouth, Massachusetts, brought him world acclaim. As author of such sea classics as CRUISE OF THE CONRAD, BY WAY OF CAPE HORN, THE WAY OF A SHIP, and THE SET OF THE SAILS (his autobiography), Mr. Villiers has made a permanent and magnificent contribution to our knowledge of the sea and sailing ships. Mr. Villiers was a technical consultant to the Louis de Rochemont organization throughout the production of WINDJAMMER.

CONTRARY to the general belief, the sailing ship is by no means finished yet. I mean the ocean-going, square-rigged ship, the classic "windjammer." A fleet of at least thirty-five such ships still goes to sea, training boys. If all these ships came sailing into the port of New York at once, they would fill every berth on the Hudson River or make South Street look again as it used to, in the 1890's. The array of graceful masts and yards, the crowd of clipper bows and adventurous jib-booms would look like Iquique in the West Coast nitrate days, or San Francisco in the Gold Rush—five four-mast barks (each over 3,000 tons); eight full-rigged ships, ranging in size from 400 to 2800 tons; fifteen barks and barkentines, at least two of the barks old Cape Horners, and two of the barkentines less than five years old; a dozen or more topsail schooners. This fleet would fly the flags of Spain, Portugal, Belgium, Brazil, Japan, Yugoslavia, Chile, Italy, the United States, Denmark, Norway, Sweden, France, Germany, Soviet Russia, Indonesia. No dying old ships, these! Many of them are comparatively new and lovely vessels, especially designed for the work they do. The Chilean four-mast barkentine *Esmeralda* and the Indonesian barkentine *Dewerutji* are almost new. Germany contemplates the building of a big bark for naval training.

Why? Why all these windjammers, in a powered age? Who wants sailing-ship sailors now? Are these ships any use for cargo-carrying? They are not. They do not lift a single ton of cargo among the lot of them. What do they do, then? How can they earn their keep? Carry dudes on yachting voyages? Hire out to film companies, serve some whim of some fabulous foreign ship-owner? They do none of these things. Not at all. The whole fleet exists for one purpose only, and that is for the indoctrination of competent youth in the age-old ways of the sea. Some are naval school-ships, some merchant marine. The United

he Sea...

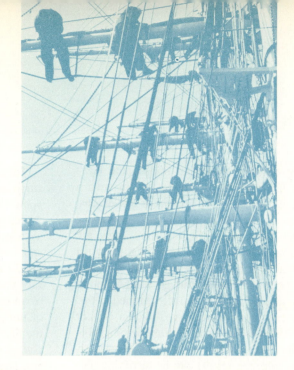

States bark *Eagle* operates entirely for the officer cadets at the U. S. Coast Guard Academy at New London. The Italian ship *Amerigo Vespucci* trains cadets for the Italian navy; the Spanish four-mast barkentine *Juan Sebastian Delcano* turns out cadets for the Spanish navy; the Danish full-rigged ship *Georg Stage* takes in eighty raw boys each spring and turns them, within the half-year, into valuable young mariners for the Danish merchant service.

Regardless of who is trained aboard, the object is the same: to provide what seamen consider to be the best possible training of all. Many of these ships are nationally supported. Some are operated by particular ports. Others are the responsibility of societies of shipowners. What they all seek is good officer material for ships at sea, and they know how to get it. Shipowners are hardheaded businessmen, forthright and competent men, and heavily taxed. They are not looking for a few sailing-ship mates and masters. What they want is an assured and regular flow of recruits of the right kind onto the bridges of their fast, costly and enormous vessels—recruits who will develop into reliable and resourceful officers and captains, dependable in the control of the vastly complicated and expensive ships which carry the world's sea-borne trade today—80,000-ton tankers, 65,000-ton ore-carriers, 40-knot passenger liners that cost anything from fifteen to fifty million dollars. No matter what gadgets may be invented or developed, radar-twiddlers and all the rest, in the last analysis it is men that count—competent, clear-sighted men,

tested in adversity, reliable under stress, possessed of the right degrees of initiative and responsibility, men who *know themselves* as well as the vocational side of the seafaring profession, and know from experience that they can do the right thing at the right time, no matter how trying the circumstances.

In the sailing ship, a young man learns by experience to dedicate himself to something greater than himself—the service of the sea. He learns, or quits. The teamwork of the sailing ship, the constant necessity to make the *right* decision upon the instant (frequently affecting life and death), the acceptance of discipline, not artificial but accepted by all as necessary for their very survival, the sharing of hardships which are unavoidable and not contrived, the true delight in finding one's own personality against the clear and clean, the windblown and unhurried background of the sailing ship at sea—all these factors play a part, unobtrusively but surely, in the development of character and the qualities of true leadership, which cannot be duplicated or even imagined in the ordinary powered vessel.

"A passage under sail brings out in the course of days whatever there may be of sea lore and sea sense in any individual whose soul is not indissolubly wedded to the pedestrian shore," wrote that great seaman, Captain Joseph Conrad.

A passage under sail—that is the thing! Not time in powered steamships, motorships, gas-turbine vessels, or atomic-powered, either. First things first—that is the way of the sea; and the windjammer puts them there. The windjammer gets right down to elemental things, and stays there. A lad must learn mighty fast in such a ship and, since he sees the reason for the lessons, he gets on with the learning. He isn't cramming knowledge. He is absorbing lore, know-how, the very soul and substance of men's fight against the sea—a fight that's not won yet, by any means, for great vessels still go missing upon ocean voyages, ill-laden and ill-trimmed, ships break in two and founder, great liners (where someone very obviously made some wrong split-second decision) still can crash into one another. When they do, the results can be terrifying, because of their very complexity and the great speed with which today's enormous ships can hurl themselves along. Sometimes things seem too easy, under power. But the illusion can be dangerous. The sea is a hard taskmaster and will remain so, no matter what may be invented or developed to lessen risks. No device, no aid— no knob-twirling fog-piercer or electronic means of establishing position—is of the slightest use if the officer gaining the knowledge doesn't use it rightly, in the moment of test.

Those sailing ships are a tough school. They're meant to be. The sea is not a calling for softies. No passenger, in an Atlantic gale or Grand Banks fog, reflects with equanimity on the academic qualifications of those on the bridge. It is their *seamanship* he trusts, implicitly. And that seamanship is best learned under sail.

Start of the Tall Ships Race off Torbay, England.

To stand alone at the wheel, feeling all the surge and power and the swift response of the *good* ship to one's slightest movement of the wheel spokes with no engine in between, to fight as a group of shipmates high aloft above the spume-filled and stormy sea bringing in some wind-stiffened, rain-sodden, gale-filled sail, to race up the weather rigging with lungs full of the clean sea air, to live for months in a ship devoid of noise and fumes and all distractions—this is the life! Risk there is, of course, for the sea will always have its dangers. Adventure there is, too, and challenge—challenge to body and to spirit.

Some of these sailing school-ships have gone down. During my career, four of them have gone. With them, 250 boys—the *Niobe, Kjøbenhavn, Karpfanger, Pamir.* The *Niobe,* blown over in a Baltic squall, caught upon a summer day with her ports open and the boys at their lessons in the schoolrooms below: the *Kjøbenhavn,* giant five-masted Dane, than which no better built windjammer ever took the sea, gone missing on a Roaring Forties run between Montevideo and Australia. *Admiral Karpfanger,* lost somewhere near Cape Horn racing homeward from Spencer Gulf with her grain; the powerful four-mast bark *Pamir,* another German school-ship, gone in a hurricane off the Azores with almost all her boys. Well, there have always been losses. It is because of the risks of the sea that seamen must be trained to face those risks and to pay the price if called upon.

We all have faced those risks, and more than once. One calls to mind specific occasions when great ships came very near to going down, suddenly, without trace. The big four-master *Herzogin Cecilie,* for example, very nearly added her name to the lists of missing ships on one passage, outward bound in ballast from Denmark toward Australia. In a sudden shifting wind, somewhere to the north of Scotland, when the ship had been at sea little more than a week, the ballast shifted down below and at once she fell upon her beam ends. The wind screamed and the sea rose, and her lee yardarms dipped in the water. How far would she go? Right over? It seemed horribly likely. For a moment, she simply hung there, motionless. She lay on her side

Photographs by the author

like a gigantic half-tide rock, half-in, half-out of the water, and the seas breaking along her weather side exposed her to the keel.

The crew were boys, twenty of them, average age seventeen. All aboard were sailing-ship men, from the thirty-three-year-old captain and twenty-two-year-old chief mate to the nineteen-year-old cook. For one terrifying moment, all hands held their breath and clung to bits of rigging with all their strength lest they go into the sea with the rolled-over ship's wild lurching.

But she hung there. She went over no further.

"Into the hold, lads!" The captain shouted.

What, into the hold, half under water? Go down *there* in the innards of the ship and be drowned when she slipped, drowned without chance to swim, without breath of fresh air, or glimpse of daylight! What sort of order was this?

To a man, all hands followed that captain immediately, taking such shovels and gear as the ship provided, down into the hold through a small hatch beneath the long poop, down into the side of the ship right below the water. Here the ballast of shingle and builders' rubbish had poured out from behind the planks which we had erected to keep it in position. Fifteen hundred tons of the stuff had moved to leeward and was slipping and sliding around as the great bark lurched in the wild and growing sea. Fifteen hundred tons! And we were twenty boys. . . .

We started at once to shovel the stuff back to

A windjammer in an Atlantic storm.

windward and secure it there. We salvaged the planks and built up a box of dunnage and old hatches to hold the ballast where we retrimmed it. Hour after hour in the great dark hold, lit by the feeble rays of a few oil lanterns, we sweated with shovels and bare hands. At first, as fast as we flung a shovelful to windward, two shovelfuls rolled back. We stood literally upon the side of the ship as if it were the bottom. It was curiously quiet and eerie down there, for the noise of the gale did not penetrate. All hatches were down and caulked (and on their strength depended our lives, and we knew that, for the sea was half-over all of them). Hour after hour, watch after watch, day after day, night after night, the twenty boys toiled down there, and it was not until the third day that we could even make out a noticeable lifting of the lee side from the boiling sea. We lost count of time. The gale still blew, for north of Scotland—between the Orkneys and wild Iceland—is a bad place for weather.

But we'd won, and we knew that. Within the week (with no rest at all, not for anyone) we had that ship upright again. Then we bent more sails, to replace those blown away in the gale. We bent more sails and carried on toward Australia. And when we came in there, after 80 days, no one ashore noticed anything. No one knew how close we had been to not coming in at all.

Under that same captain, years afterward, in another giant of a four-mast bark called *Parma* (from the same line as the *Pamir*) we had a mighty close call again. Nothing but the immediate response of the boy-crew to their orders and the great hearts of the sailing-ship crew brought us to the morning. The *Parma* was a heavy ship, carrying a great press of sail, and we were driving her toward Cape Horn in the Grain Race from Australia. Then a sea swept over her, from aft—a great breaking curling mountainous brute of a sea roaring from the murk astern, driven by the violent and ever-increasing gale that shrieked and screamed in all the spume-soaked rigging and flung itself like a tormented and solid mass upon the distended black shapes of the driving sails, strained to the utmost! A pooping sea, the worst kind of sea—

a killing sea, a murderer! No one saw it coming. Until then, we had run all right. It was wild and dangerous weather, but no worse than the usual Cape Horn gale. It was fair wind, in our favor. All we had to do was to run before it to survive. Seas creamed the decks from rail to rail, burst upon the high coamings of the well-protected hatches, smashed against bulkheads, capstans, houses, boats. All this was normal.

But a pooping sea was not normal at all. The ship must keep her poop above the seas at all times for her brains were there—her brains, in the shape of her captain and his afterguard; her controls, in the shape of binnacle and wheel. The pooping sea roared over her. Up and up she rose, but never high enough! Down crashed the sea, down fell the ship! When the sea had cleared a little from the poop, rushing forward onto the main deck like a flood upon a cateract, the steering compasses were gone. The helmsman had lost control of the steering. The ship took a wild lurch, *across* the wind and sea, fell into the trough, broached to!

In plain language, our four-masted bark was absolutely out of control, for the sea swept right over her as she lay and wallowed and, with a frightening and frightful tumult, the black shapes of her too-big sails flapped and thundered at their restraining sheets and robands and at the steel yards, as if they were trying with the utmost effort and mad desperation to bring all the rigging about our ears. If those steel masts and spars came down, there would be no morning! No morning ever again for us. We knew that. They would flail in the decks, start the steel sides, let the water into us and down we would go. She could stand water on deck, but not in the hold.

We had no radio. There was no other ship within a thousand miles, save the *Pamir,* and she was fighting for her life in the same storm.

One look aloft showed all holding there, for the time being—all holding except some of the sails, which had taken one wild flap and flown off in ribbons like jet-propelled albatrosses before the gale. The ship rolled violently. Strips of blown-out canvas, writhing buntline wires and ends of chain screamed and thundered aloft.

"Get the main tops'l off!" roared the captain.

What, go aloft up there, in that madhouse of hell? Climb up against the gale and fight upward against the rolling, leaping motion of the demented, uncontrollable ship, among the maddened, contorted chains and wire, and fight sail?

Upon the instant, figures clambered into the weather rigging, in swift obedience. We went, all of us. We fought the sails through that wild night, while the officers fought the helm and, with the aid of the patent Scots brace winches which our *Parma* had, brought the ship out of the trough and hove to. That is to say, she no longer rolled hopelessly in the belly of the raging sea, flinging her mastheads in a long arc; she came out of the trough, shoulder to the sea, and lay there with the few sails that were left braced properly, holding her, keeping her just in the one place, no longer trying to fight the sea but drifting leewards, yielding. No longer did the seas leap over us, though it was still hellish up aloft and it took all night to get the rags of the main topsail in. Hove to, we were saved, so long as ice kept out of our way....

The Joseph Conrad.

Again our crew were boys—twenty-four all told, and the average age, seventeen.

That was years ago. Now many of those boys are liner masters, not only at sea. Two are captains of transatlantic air liners. They all did well.

We found out long afterward, when we came into port, that the *Pamir* also sailed through hell that night, but neither suffered any damage, nor lost a boy. She was a magnificent ship, exceptionally strongly built.

Yet the sea took the *Pamir* too, in due course. Coming up with grain from the River Plate for Hamburg in the fall of '57, a vicious North Atlantic hurricane recurved on her and knocked her down. She had radio, then—radio, a big auxiliary Diesel (which we had never had), a crowd of boys. But she went, just the same. Her captain tried to race across the hurricane's face to get on the right side of it and keep his big ship safe. He almost got away with it—almost. Not quite. But his very daring contributed to the disaster, for his ship would have been better off hove to; and the very strength of the big *Pamir* helped her downfall too. She had too much sail set, and they would not come down. Unlike our *Parma* broaching to, the sails did not blow away. Our *Parma* had stood up and her cargo had not shifted, for it was all in carefully stowed sacks. The *Pamir's* was loose, and shifted, holding her down, as the hurricane screamed upon her. Over, over she went, until her yardarms dipped in the sea and the breaking water along her weather side exposed her to the keel, while the lee side was beneath the sea. Boats? All smashed! Maybe she would float, even though on her side. Other sailing ships had. But the *Pamir* was vulnerable, for the necessary air intakes, and the ventilation for the engine, and the means of access to the unusual amount of accommodation down below had, by their very existence, left spaces where the sea could get in. (In our *Parma,* no water could get below unless the hatches went, or the falling yards smashed us first, and they had stood.)

The *Pamir* was doomed, once the water was inside her. She would go right over, and slip down. . . . It took the greater part of a dreadful day for the big school-ship to slide under the sea.

Fortunately, we knew what happened in this case. From the *Kjøbenhavn* and the *Karpfanger,* no one survived to tell the story. From the *Pamir,* six boys were snatched out of the sea, adrift in waterlogged and broken boats.

I have talked with some of these. The picture that emerges is not only one of catastrophe. As the *Pamir* went over, over, toward her death, the boy-crew and the seasoned sailors continued at their work together, doing what they could, fighting the canvas, trying to trim the yards, doing their best to get back some control over the dying ship. They worked in water to their necks. As the ship rolled sluggishly, ever farther and farther over on the lee side, the water often closed right over them. They worked on, all of them, until she slipped right down below the tormented surface of the dreaful sea and was gone from them. Gone from them, and the spume that filled the wind-maddened air filled their lungs, and there was little chance to swim. Their dedication to the service of the sea, learned under sail, stayed with them to the last. . . .

No one launched boats. Broken hulls of the boats drifted off by themselves, and the survivors somehow miraculously found themselves in them. There, adrift, searching vessels rescued them, after many days.

Now they are at sea again, all six; for that is the spirit of the sea, learned in that great school of the sea, the sailing ship.

Under full sail.

A hazard of life
as a mess boy.

Voyage of the Christian Radich

Notes from the Diary of One of the Cadets Recorded by William Terry

November 11th: I want to go to sea with all my heart! In Norway, nobody ever lives very far from the sea and most Norwegian boys feel the same way I do Today is the longest day in my life because tomorrow my fate will be decided. I keep thinking about tomorrow's competition when hundreds of boys will apply but only forty-five will be chosen for the greatest adventure of a lifetime. It was only two weeks ago that Grandfather read me the announcement in the paper about the special cruise the *Christian Radich* will make to the West Indies and ports in the United States. Father had said if I wanted to go on a training cruise badly enough, I would have to work after school to make my tuition fee. But the winners of tomorrow's competition will be awarded training scholarships — and have all that fun besides!

Horten, November 12th: I caught the first bus to Oslo. As I expected, there were hundreds of boys from every corner of Norway with the same keen desire as mine. They were all big and strong and we fell into conversation easily while waiting. Finally it was my turn before the selection committee. I met the interviewers' searching scrutiny as squarely as I could. Their ability to uncover my weaknesses and my strong points was uncanny. Tonight, I'm back home in Horten; outwardly assured, inwardly stepping lightly on thin ice.

Horten, November 20th: I've spent nine awful days of waiting and watching the mail. Out of the five hundred boys who applied, only forty-

five will be chosen. I can't possibly be one of them.

Horten, November 21st: I am going! The letter came at 2 P.M. I couldn't believe my eyes, and it was only after the whole family took turns in congratulating me and reading and re-reading the letter that the words began to sink in. I am to go! On a true sailing ship, to be trained for the third largest merchant-marine fleet in the world!

Oslo, December 6th: After reporting on board to the First Mate, Nils Arnsten, I was sent below deck for assignment by the Sergeant. The first thing he did was to give me a number —a number I would be known by for the next nine months. I learned that on a sailing ship they use the number system for several reasons. Numbers are easier to remember than names; they simplify the watch system—even numbers are members of the port watch, odd, starboard. Finally, a boy's number designates what mast and yardarm are to be his position when going aloft. Next came the issuing of uniforms and hammock. Laden with a small mountain of goods, I made my way forward to the 'tween-decks compartment. This will be the dormitory, mess hall and recreation room for all forty-five of us. It is only forty-five feet by 30—with six big picnic-style tables and benches. The bulk-heads are lined with lockers for each boy's personal belongings. However, the hammocks are unhooked and stored during the day, so there is really much more room than appeared at first. While I was stowing my gear I got acquainted with some of my shipmates, a couple of whom I remembered from the day of the interview. One of them showed us the proper method of getting into a swing hammock. He grasped the overhead steel beam and, with complete confidence, hoisted himself up and over. What happened next was lost in a blur of arms and legs. When it was all over he lay on the deck, dazed, looking as if he had been put through a threshing machine.

Oslo, December 8th (late afternoon): We heard the shrill blast of the Bosun's pipe ordering us on deck. We lined up, in our new uniforms, standing at attention. Our Captain is exactly what I always imagined a sailing-ship master would look like: stocky, well built, with a penetrating look in his slate-blue eyes that leaves no doubt that he is a man of action and a man to be depended upon in an emergency at sea. He is approaching his seventieth birthday, but looks fifteen years younger. Stepping to the edge of the poop deck, he said: "Training you to become good sailors is the primary mission of this cruise. All of you have been handpicked and we expect you to live up to our requirements. All you have to do is obey orders and do your duty like men. If we pull together you will find me a decent fellow; if we don't, you will find me something quite different." We continued to stand at attention for an inspection by officials and Crown Prince Olav [Now His Majesty, King Olav V of Norway] who had come down to wish us fair winds and good sailing. Then the ceremony was over. After a hug from Mother and a firm handshake from Father, the moment had come. Under dark, gray, snow-laden skies, our ship nosed out into the cold waters of Oslofjord.

Skagerrak, first day out of Oslo: We have a friendly little hound on board that somebody named Stump. All sailing ships used to have mascots, but I don't believe any ever had a piano for one of the crew members. Ours does. We have fastened Sven Erik's piano in the 'tween-decks compartment. He is supposed to practice (Father's orders) but not when we sleep (Captain's command). The officers have not lost a minute in beginning our training. At first glance the rigging of a windjammer is a complete maze of lines, blocks and cables. It doesn't make any sense at all. The A. B. who took charge of my class group was a gruff but pleasant fellow named Lasse Kolstad, who said: "Your lily-white hands may feel a bit tender at first, but we'll toughen 'em up in short order." Our ship will remain in the vicinity of the south coast of Norway for a few days so that we'll have a thorough basic training before heading out to sea.

Skagerrak, 2nd day: We've been learning all about the rigging and gear. What was a confusing mystery is becoming a beautiful arrangement of steel yards, lines and sails. It is all wonderfully co-ordinated to take full advantage of the wind. I guess it took centuries to develop such an efficient and graceful ship.

Skagerrak, 3rd day: Today I climbed into the rigging for the first time. My ship's number automatically assigned me to the yard of the upper topsail on the foremast. Upon the command, "Stand by!", we ran to the foot of the shrouds. "Entre Opp!" from the Mate sent us scrambling up the ratlines. Up I went until I reached the upper topsail yard; then, inching my way out on the single footrope below the yard, I arrived at my position. As I leaned forward to grasp the line which kept the furled sail snug against the yard, I looked down at the deck far below. A wave of dizziness broke over me. The motion of the ship, rather gentle on deck, was very marked way up there. I tried to remember "one hand for the ship and one hand for yourself," but I really needed more hands. The footrope I had been using so easily a few moments before now seemed like a thread. I had to fight back a feeling of plunging into the midst of the tiny figures on the deck. I turned my head, forcing myself to look at the boy a little farther along the yard. He

"Sketches by Pedro, 1957, aboard Christian Radich *entering New York."*

The bow lookout.

Way out on the jib boom a staysail is attended to.

A precarious perch on a lifeboat.

Hanging onto the manrope in mountainous seas.

Photo by Gerhard Gundersen

Port-of-Spain Police Band.

And mounted officers.

"I'm a sailor born to roam, while **Kari waits for me.**"

Painting ship is a never-ending task.

must have felt every bit as awful as I did, but he, at least, managed to grin at me. I felt that if I had to go, I would at least go trying, and I set to the task of unfurling the sail. By the time the command was heard: "Let go sail," my fear of the mast height was under control.

English Channel, 5th day: We've headed out into the open sea. Shipboard life and duties have become quite familiar and natural. The roughest part to get used to was the continual routine of four hours on watch and four hours off. Our appetites are fierce. The slop chest doesn't have any more chocolate—just hard candies.

Bay of Biscay, 11th day: The weather was very cold today as we prepared to celebrate Christmas. An increasingly heavy sea began pounding our bow. We had to go aloft to shorten sail for safety's sake. I was thankful to have "learned the ropes" in calm waters. What was not properly secured below decks was sliding around crazily—watched in misery by those who were discovering what acute seasickness is really like. The filthy weather has blown into a real gale.

Bay of Biscay, 13th day: Sven Erik has been practicing Grieg's A Minor Concerto. This morning we had to run a line to hold Sven Erik as well as the piano to the deck. I'm already a little tired of the tune, but topside it is good to hear the music coming through the wind scoop.

Off Portugal, 18th day: Just have not been up to writing. Perhaps it's better to gloss over unpleasant things and so I will simply note that during the preceding days our ship, with all sails secured and red storm lanterns displayed to notify other ships that we could not maneuver, lay wallowing in mountainous waves—often being blown *back* over twenty miles a day. These have been the most terrible days I have ever known. Lasse said that the great ocean liner *Ile de France* was forced back to port by the storm we have weathered. Maybe we are becoming windjammer men after all.

Madeira, 37th day: A wonderful thing happens this afternoon. It has become suddenly warm, like spring in Horten. I saw Per start up the foremast shrouds with a red bundle under his arm. I followed him up to the royal yard. When he reached the top, he loosened the bun-

dle—it was his long red underwear—and he let it float out into the sea! I looked down—everyone on deck was standing at attention as the underwear drifted away. Then I looked forward—and Per and I could see our first landfall, Madeira! A mountain sticking out of the sea into some clouds. The boys on deck couldn't see "around the earth" yet—but they all hurried up to look. Zarco, the Portuguese explorer saw the island in 1419—he couldn't have been happier than we were. Tomorrow we anchor in Funchal!

South Atlantic, 39th day: From Madeira we are following the 1492 route of Columbus. We are bound "towards" San Juan, Puerto Rico. If this were a steamship, they would say "bound for"—but with sailing ships, you never know. The Trade Winds are giving us an opportunity to apply a long overdue beauty treatment to our ship. From the tip of the masts down to the waterline, she is getting a facelifting. Painting the long cables that brace the masts is a challenge. To tackle them you have to put your trust in a bosun's chair—a section of plank just big enough to sit on and encircled with a stout line. The chair runs through a block near the very top of the mast. This enables you to be lowered down the length of the cable, painting as you go. This afternoon, as I was suspended high over the poop working on the mizzenmast cable, a greater than usual roll to port caught me unprepared. I grabbed the cable with one hand, and with the other, clutched the chair. Of course I forgot about the wildly swinging bucket of paint hanging on the underside of the chair, and most of the contents went slopping downward. It missed the Captain by inches. His calm look went from the mess at his feet to my face, and down again to the splattered paint. After a long pause, he simply said, "So, so," and walked away to the charthouse. I was rapidly lowered in the chair and found myself in front of the Bosun—who had plenty to say. But I did a perfect cleanup job. I just hope the Captain remembers that he was a deck boy too—once.

South by West Canary Islands, 41st day: I don't know what to write down about our meeting with the German four-mast bark, *Pamir*. She was sighted from the poop deck by Sven, on the stern lookout, that is, her topgallants and upper-topsails were sighted. Lasse climbed the mizzenmast and was able to see her black hull. She was altering course and sailing toward us. Neither the Captain nor any of the mates had ever had such a chance encounter with another windjammer in open waters. She is a beautiful ship—we've been sailing together—shouting greetings to the cadets on board. She's carrying cargo to Montivideo, Uruguay. This has been a wonderful experience.

Mid-Atlantic, 48th day: This evening the Bosun told us how Captain Kjelstrup and the *Christian Radich* won the Tall Ships Race from Tor Bay to Lisbon. It seems that the *Radich* pulled way out in front of all the other deep-sea ships at the start. Then at dusk she was becalmed, her position way west. The radio announcer said it seemed she had given up and was heading for America. The weather reports said that a southeast wind would come up in the morning, and this would have been terrible for our ship—120 miles off Lisbon. However, the Captain looked at the clouds and saw no sign of a southeast wind. In fact, at 3:30 A.M. the wind came up from the south-*west* and, after coming about, the *Radich* was pushed straight across the finish line—twenty-three hours ahead of all the other square-riggers which had run into headwinds. The Captain's experience and seamanship won the race.

San Juan, 56th day: This has been our first contact with Americans. It's been wonderful. Parties and invitations all over the place. Most exciting for me was the visit to the Governor's Palace, Fortaleza. I had heard of Pablo Casals, but I didn't really want to go with Sven Erik and Kaare—all cello music had to be dull. But Mr. Casals is different! He looks like Mr. Soordheim—the banker in his gray suit—but when he started to play, I never wanted to leave.

Mid-Caribbean (enroute Curacao) 61st day: Every day there is something new to remember "forever." Now in the tropics we all sleep topside at night. I can watch the blue-black sails swing back and forth across the deep blue sky, filled layer upon layer with stars. We have a good wind, although it is quite calm and we're making 8 knots. I'm not in heaven, because in a few hours the sun will be up and I'll be scrubbing the decks. But I can almost picture

heaven out here. I feel so big and so small—all at the same time.

South Caribbean, 63rd day: Lost our log line today. A shark was seen following in our wake, but before the second cook could get superstitious about the shark being there to collect a dead man, the big fish bit off the propeller on the end of the line and disappeared. Now we will have to depend upon the Captain and the mates hearing the "sing" of the water to know how far and how fast we are sailing during a four-hour watch. Lasse found a shark hook and padded it with meat from the galley, but no one has seen any fins, and so far he's had no luck.

Willemstad, 65th day: I guess our Captain is about as good as those ancient Vikings who could tell their position by the color of the water. His dead reckoning brought us right close to Curaçao's harbor. Sailing up the "main street," we could almost talk to the Dutch on either side of the channel. They seemed excited about seeing a windjammer. The Norwegian Seamen's Church called special greetings to us in Norwegian, and we both dipped our colors. Right now, we're not so happy—tomorrow we start to scrape the bottom of the ship.

Leaving Willemstad, 70th day: No time for notes once the scraping and painting were finished. Curaçao was fun. Those Dutch girls are charming. Yesterday we all had a big picnic—a *rijstuffel* they call it—on an old estate. Even Stump went on liberty—unofficial—but he proved he was a real sea dog by rejoining us. I know he met a friend in Willemstad. Now he's sitting on the poop deck looking back, longingly, I think. His whiskers have been flattened back by the wind for so long, they now grow that way. Somehow, no matter how much I enjoyed being in a port, I always start feeling better when we are headed out. Is this being a seaman, or having a ship for a home?

Mid-Caribbean, 77th day: Seven days out of Curaçao and we are becalmed, with the current against us. We've all been so excited about getting to Trinidad that the change in the weather has made us grumpy. The heat and humidity haven't helped, either. The doldrums have put the whole ship out of kilter—not just the sails. Superstitions most of us had scoffed at are now finding many earnest believers.

Splicing a steel cable.

In frogman's gear for underwater shooting.

The Cinemiracle camera shoots the CHRISTIAN RADICH
scudding along under full sail.

Celeste Holm comes aboard in New York to find out if Kjell Holm (#30) of Norvasund is a distant cousin.

CHRISTIAN RADICH cadets on the Capitol steps, with Senator Wiley.

The Portuguese naval school-ship SAGRES.

The U. S. Coast Guard windjammer EAGLE sailing at full speed.

After all, we left Curacao on a Friday. . . . If I whistle the right tune, close my eyes and scratch the windward side of the mast, will it bring us a wind? Sven Erik's practicing on that Grieg Concerto may be driving away the wind. . . .

Charlotte Amalie, Virgin Islands, 80th day: What a wonderful evening! Am writing this by the moonlight—it is so bright. We are still waiting for the right winds to take us on to Trinidad. A funny thing happened earlier this evening. We had a swell beach party—complete with native drummers, pretty girls and a song fest. But after that, I had the night watch. Just after three bells, some splashes attracted my attention. It was the "Doctor" [the cook's traditional name aboard sailing ships] along with two others who had missed the last boat back to the ship. Sverre had come to get a dory and row back for the others. He was nearly spent when he reached the ship. He had tried to make the distance from shore to ship in one burst of speed because he knew that the waters through which he swam are supposed to be alive with shark and barracuda . . . the moon is beginning to set now and I can hear my relief coming up the ladder.

Port-of-Spain, 86th day: Before we first went ashore here, the Captain reminded us that the purpose of this voyage was not to give us a good time—we are supposed to learn, to meet people and understand a little about the world. There does seem to be something remarkable about Trinidad—it has so many people that I would have called different—English, Spanish, Negro, Indian, and East Indian, Dutch, Chinese—but they are all Trinidadians. Everyone has been very friendly to us, and this Calypso is really fun. It's catching. When reporting back aboard, I nearly replied to the Third Mate: "Yes, man, yes, indeed."

Off Florida, 116th day: Maybe it's just wishful thinking, but some of the boys coming off watch swear they can see neon lights on the American shore. There was one startling light we did see for sure. After sundown, the sky was clear. We noticed a strange grouping of very bright stars. The Second Mate explained that it was the large comet that the radio said would be visible in our latitude. There it was, suspended in space, apparently motionless—but we knew it to be roaring through space with a fiery tail extending hundreds of thousands of miles behind it.

New York, 126th day: Kjell, who has relatives in Brooklyn, invited us to a dance at the Norwegian-American Society in Brooklyn. All the people we met there had real Norwegian names, and the girls looked as if they had stepped out of an Oslo school, but their Norwegian had a Brooklyn accent. A few of my shipmates didn't get there until it was almost over. A group led by Harald had started off, armed with a set of directions and a complete subway map. Harald had just finished his tour in the Army before we left Oslo and he was sure he could read any map. That is, until he arrived at the station where three subway lines converged. By the time the train they selected was passing the Yankee Stadium, they realized they'd better ask for help, otherwise they would have missed it all.

New York, 130th day: I haven't written much about the ship's work that has to go on while we are in port. There is always a lot of it. Today we have been bending on the heavy suit of storm sails for our trip back across the North Atlantic. All the older canvas is stowed away, except for some foresails the sailmaker is mending. New York is a challenging city. I don't think I'd like to be lonely here, but there's so much to do and see.

Off New England with the U.S. Navy, 193rd day: Today I was on board the *U.S.S. Manley*, navy destroyer. We had a complete tour, beginning at the radar masts and ending in the engine room. Then we were all assigned to duty with the sea detail. I helped chip and "redlead" a hatch, but all the time I had to answer the American sailors' questions about life aboard a square-rigger. They all thought I was very lucky—and I guess a windjammer is *really* the way to learn about the sea.

Off Portsmouth, New Hampshire, 208th day: We are on our way home with a fair, cold wind, but it will take a lot more than cold air to cool off our excitement after yesterday's performance by Sven Erik Libaek of the Grieg Concerto with Arthur Fiedler and the Boston Pops Orchestra. The rest of us had forgotten about Sven Erik's resolve to audition for Mr. Fiedler, and we *never* expected the maestro to bring the whole orchestra to the dock! We were proud of

Sven Erik, proud of our ship, proud of our country—and very proud of the friendships we have made in America.

North Atlantic, 224th day: Another day of fog. After ten straight days of foul weather we should be used to it. The member of the ship's company taking it hardest is Stump. He can't endure the endless moaning of the foghorn. Now he spends most of the time below decks looking as if he doesn't have a friend in the world. We all seem to be living in the past, these days. This evening we were looking over each other's souvenirs—recalling the things we did together.

Off the South Coast of Norway, 237th day: The lights of Norway at last! Tomorrow this compartment I have shared with forty-four others, this hammock I'm now so comfortable in, this ship I've come to love—will become a

memory. I'm not so anxious to be home, now.

Oslo, 238th day: Our ship received a grand welcome all the way up Oslofjord. We were escorted by two magnificent windjammers, the Danish *Danmark,* and our own *Sørlandet.* I could see Father and Mother on the pier. . . . We were home again! It was good to greet them both! They say I've grown—and I guess I have. So much has happened to me during these months away. Tomorrow we will sign off, and my parents will want to know all about the voyage. I will have plenty of stories —but where to begin? Maybe with the *Pamir.* . . . Her sinking is a tragedy. We were unsinkable—or so we thought—and we would have stuck to our lines the way her boys did—I really believe this. Maybe that is a good place to begin. One thing I know, I hope twenty years from now there will be a sailing schoolship—I'd like to send my boy out on it.

CAPTAIN YNGVAR KJELSTRUP. Captain Yngvar Kjelstrup, skipper of the *Christian Radich,* is dean of Norway's sailing masters. He was born in Hoenefoss, a small town near Oslo, and made his first trip to sea at the age of fifteen when he ran away to Glasgow, Scotland, and signed up on the Norwegian Cape Horner, *Alacrita.* He is proud of his Viking ancestry and there have been sailors in his family for generations. He is a graduate of Norway's Naval Academy and saw active service in both World Wars. He has been decorated seven times, including a decoration from General Eisenhower for the part he played in assisting the Allies during our invasion of Europe. He became master of the *Christian Radich,* which he built in 1937, and took the windjammer to sea for the Cinemiracle cameras in his seventieth year.

OFFICERS AND CREW OF THE CHRISTIAN RADICH

OFFICERS

Captain Yngvar Kjelstrup
1st Officer Nils Arntsen
2nd Officer Oscar Strønen
3rd Officer Semund Remøy
Chief Engineer Nils Hermansen
Doctor Gunnulv Hauge

MEN

Sergeant Harmvild Landstad
1st Bosun Asbjørn Espenak
2nd Bosun Arian Fredriksen
Motorman Arne Andersen
Steward Sverre Solheim
1st Cook Eric Sandbach
2nd Cook Knut Iversen
Sailmaker Sigurd Borgen
1st A. B. Gunnar Haugsvaer
2nd A. B. Trygve Bendiksen
3rd A. B. Lasse Kolstad

*The number that appears before each boy's name is his "Watch Number." On a sailing ship these numbers are used by Officers and Petty Officers, rather than the boys' names, because the number is easily remembered and simpler to write in the watch book when assigning duties.

BOYS — Starboard Watch*

1. Bjørn Sandbech (Bø-i-Telemark)
3. Tor Markussen (Oslo)
5. Bjørn Amvik (Hvalstad)
7. Arild Kristoffersen (Oslo)
9. Johan Egeland (Kvinesdal)
11. Jørgen Lanes (Stathelle)
13. Tormod Tofteland (Kristiansand)
15. Fred Hegerstrøm (Oslo)
17. Otto Snildal (Tofte-i-Hurum)
19. Tor Rue (Flatdal)
21. Per Antonsen (Kopervik)
23. Svein Aske (Trondheim)
25. Peer Dahl (Drammen)
27. Egil Sandnes (Dalsøyra)
29. Jan Høyberg (Aalesund)
31. Even Børresen (Kongsvinger)
33. Per Johnsen (Oslo)
35. Sven Erik Libaek (Oslo)
71. Ola Maerk (Tynset)
73. Kjell Kristensen (Rjukan)
81. Stein Petterson (Sarpsborg)
83. Thormod Saglien (Askim)
85. Tore Bilet (Sarpsborg)

BOYS — Port Watch*

2. Kaare Terland (Egersund)
4. Leiv Fornes (Nord Trondelag)
6. Reidar Kjelstrup (Oslo)
8. Frithjof Thoresen (Bodø)
10. Geir Ivar Nustad (Ringebu)
12. Olav Knudsen (Ski)
14. Tor Fossnes (Asker)
16. Jon Reistad (Løten)
18. Carl Robert Pihl (Molde)
20. Harry Guttersrud (Sørumsand)
22. Edvard Hokland (Melbu)
24. Frode Ringheim (Voss)
26. Hans Tandberg (Sande)
28. Jan Christiansen (Nyksund)
30. Kjell Holm (Aalesund)
32. Harald Tusberg (Bergen)
34. Jan Halvorsen (Oslo)
70. Audun Heggertveit (Hjelmaas)
72. Per Kirkaune (Eidsvoll)
80. Bjørn Owren (Trondheim)
82. Tor-Arne Strømmen (Namsos)
84. Thor Dalelv (Aalesund)

Our boys aboard the OLD IRONSIDES.

All Scandinavia salutes the safe return of WINDJAMMER.

Our WINDJAMMER passes the Cinemiracle camera crew on the deck of a U. S. Navy submarine.

Photo by Cadet Sven Erik Libaek

A U. S. Navy task force sighted from the bow of the CHRISTIAN RADICH.

Death of the Pamir. Captain Alan Villiers' radio broadcast over the BBC, September 21, 1957:

"The German sailing school-ship *Pamir,* 3,100 tons, is reported in distress in the wake of Hurricane Carrie, about 600 miles southwest of the Azores. Messages received from the ship indicate that the vessel is lying on her side with her sails blown away, and the foremast is broken. There are variously reported to be eighty-six to ninety-three men and boys on board, including fifty-five cadets. Most of these cadets are on their first voyage to sea. The U. S. Coast Guard cutter *Absecon* and other vessels, including several German steamships, are searching for the *Pamir,* but bad visibility with driving rain and high seas is adding to the difficulties of the search."

At 11:15 A.M., the *Pamir,* stripped of all her sails, and badly battered by the force of the hurricane winds, rolled slowly over and sank. Out of her crew of eighty-six men and boys, only six were saved.

The Viking Sword

King Olav with
Captain Kjelstrup.

President Eisenhower
with Midshipman.

IN OSLO, NORWAY, on a cold, clear December morning in 1956, a motorcade swept through the city toward the waterfront, turned onto a pier and drew up alongside the square-rigged school-ship, *Christian Radich*.

Out of the leading limousine stepped the then Crown Prince Olav of Norway, soon to become King Olav V. Aboard the windjammer, forty-five cadets in winter blues stood at attention in two perfectly straight rows, while their skipper, Captain Yngvar Kjelstrup, stood ramrod-straight at the gangway.

The Crown Prince was piped aboard and a double ceremony got under way. First, the Crown Prince bade the ship and its crew Godspeed as it left on its Cinemiracle adventure. Then he turned over to Captain Kjelstrup a Viking sword over a thousand years old, a sword discovered in the grave of an early Viking warrior. Its surface is deeply pitted from centuries of burial in a peat-bog not far from Oslo, and the silver and garnet overlays with which Scandinavian weapons of the Middle Ages were usually mounted have long since disappeared. Archeologists come across such weapons now and again in the graves of the Norse sailor-warriors who manned the graceful, high-prowed vessels we know as Viking ships. There is every reason to conjecture that the owner of the *Radich* sword carried it to the New World when he visited the coasts of what someday would be known as the United States and Canada. The sword was to be presented on permanent loan to the people of the United States in the name of the people of Norway. On permanent loan, because Norwegian law forbids the sale or gift of ancient relics outside the boundaries of Norway.

Shortly after the ceremony, the *Christian Radich* was on its way, and seven months later she arrived in New York. Captain Kjelstrup, accompanied by an honor guard of four cadets, journeyed with the sword to Washington, D. C. There the President's Naval Aide, Captain Evan P. Aurand, U.S.N., accepted the sword on behalf of President Eisenhower in a White House ceremony witnessed by the Honorable Wilhelm Morgenstierne, longtime Norwegian Ambassador to the United States.

The following day President Eisenhower presented the sword to the U. S. Naval Academy, and it is now on display at the Academy's museum in Annapolis.

And so the sword has returned to the land its ancient owner first gazed upon a thousand years ago.

1600 B. C: Egyptian Vessel, oar and sail propelled. Steered by two Sweeps.

900 A. D: Norse Viking Craft - one Sweep for steering - on Starboard (Steerboard) side.

Wind, Steam and Atoms

A glance at the development of ships through the ages.

1540: A Venetian Galley - rowed by war prisoners and later, convicts.

1837: S. S. Great Western, English ship, first built to steam across the Atlantic.

1951: S. S. United States, fastest ship in the world, holder of Atlantic Blue Riband.

1340: One of first ships (English) with Sternpost Rudder.

1492: Christopher Columbus' "Santa Maria".

1797: Famous "Old Ironsides", the U. S. Frigate "Constitution".

1787: John Fitch's Delaware River craft, speed two m. p. h.

1955: U. S. Atom Submarine "Nautilus".

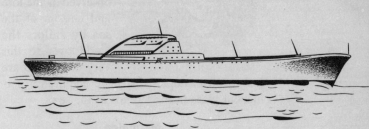

1960: Projected U. S. Atomic Merchantman.

Old Salts

It is no easy matter to trace the origins of the superstitions and folklore of the sea. But we can safely assume that from the time that man first launched his primitive boats to explore the unknown watery wastes around him a mythology of the sea began to take form.

Ignorance and fear, of course, strongly reinforced by the religious practices and superstitious beliefs of their native lands were the sources upon which men drew to create a means of coping with the real or imagined phenomena they encountered.

In the early days of sail, mariners could never be sure that they would ever see home again, once they ventured forth. To allay their doubts and terrors, natural occurrences were translated into portents of good or evil. As man's knowledge of the sea grew, a good many of his fears vanished, together with some of the earliest superstitions affecting his life at sea. But an amazingly large number of them have been accepted and scrupulously observed as the lore and custom of the sea by sailors the world over to this very day. Here are just a few examples that have acquired a permanent place in the legends of the sea.

Mermaids

These non-existent half-woman, half-fish creatures of the sea had their origin in Greek fables and, over the centuries, became a reality to all the imaginative and probably homesick men who spent very long and lonely months at sea.

The Flying Dutchman

Naturally the sailors of different lands have developed different variations on all maritime legends. The most commonly accepted version of *The Flying Dutchman* is the one about its captain who was forever condemned to rove the seas without ever touching land because he had alienated the sea gods. It is an ill omen to see this phantom ship. One can readily understand how superstitious sailors, peering into banks of fog and mist,  are certain to spot the ghostly shape of *The Flying Dutchman* bearing down upon them.

Davy Jones' Locker

This superstition began, perhaps, with the belief that a sailor lost at sea eventually found his resting place in a sea chest at the bottom of the sea. In modern times, seamen, in referring to Davy Jones' locker, simply mean the grave of all those who perish at sea.

Superstitions about Time, Weather and Omens

No sailors wanted to sail on a Friday for to do so was to invite disaster at sea. And plenty of impressive statistics can be produced to show that many vessels that did sail on a Friday went down.

Scratching the mast was supposed to encourage the wind gods to fill the sails with wind and speed the vessel toward its goal.

Almost everyone knows the saying: "Red sky

Superstitions

at night, sailors' delight, red sky at morning, sailors take warning." Strangely enough, this usually works out, proving that sometimes superstitions are based on facts deduced from observation.

A sky filled with hundreds of small puffy ridges of clouds was known as a mackerel sky,  and this was a warning of rain within 24 hours, while the sight of sea birds flying inland was a portent of storms at sea.

The Sargasso Sea, a relatively calm area in the Caribbean, is covered for miles with seaweed which, in some spots, piles up into veritable islands. Old-time sailors believed that this was the graveyard of ships, with all the currents in the world converging on this one spot, bringing all disabled and sinking vessels with them. Seamen avoided this area like the plague.

Sharks following a ship meant that there would soon be a death aboard.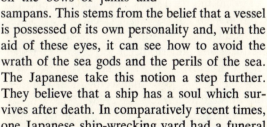

In the Orient it is a common practice to paint eyes on the bows of junks and sampans. This stems from the belief that a vessel is possessed of its own personality and, with the aid of these eyes, it can see how to avoid the wrath of the sea gods and the perils of the sea. The Japanese take this notion a step further. They believe that a ship has a soul which survives after death. In comparatively recent times, one Japanese ship-wrecking yard had a funeral service for all the ships which had come to their final resting place in this yard.

The practice of touching wood for luck originated at sea. Since a sailor had nothing but a few beams of timber between himself and the ocean, this would seem to be an obvious superstition to develop among seamen.

Sailors joining a ship would carry salt in their pockets as a symbol of good luck, while many shipbuilders would place a sprinkling of salt between the ship's timbers to help preserve them.  Often, a coin would be placed under the mast to bring good luck.

To lose a mop or bucket at sea was a sign of bad luck, while a sure sign of catastrophe was the loss or damage of a ship's flag.

In the days before the universe was understood as it is today, the appearance of a comet was the harbinger of good luck.

The sight of St. Elmo's light over the masthead would spread panic among a crew because they believed it was the souls of drowned seamen trying to board the ship.

A very cruel manifestation of superstition was based on the belief that to rescue a drowning man was to frustrate the wishes of the sea gods and bring their wrath upon the rescuer.

Some of the old beliefs are still observed today. Everyone is familiar with the custom of breaking a bottle of wine on a ship's bow at a launching, or having an animal aboard as mascot. Both these practices are supposed to bring good luck.

Old or new, founded on ignorance, fear or actual fact, the folklore of the sea adds color and romance to the mechanical age we live in.

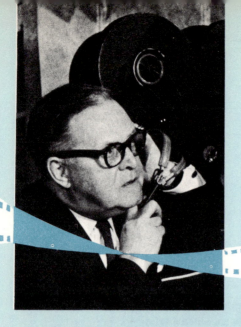

MARCH OF TIME · FIGHTING LADY · HOUSE ON 92nd STREET · BOOMERANG · CINERAMA HOLIDAY

Louis de Rochemont

ALL OF Louis de Rochemont's films have one thing in common: they bear the imprint of a *style* that is truly his own. His "real life" dramas are based on fact and are cast, for the most part, with real people pictured in their habitual environment. Thus the audience is permitted an intimate view of a story and an experience based on an actual event. The camera, rather than the professional actor, is his star. It is the "eye" of the motion picture, and he will not debase it by attempting to foist a synthetic story or setting on his audience.

Louis de Rochemont is ideally suited to the task of producing a story like WINDJAMMER. In addition to his long experience with motion pictures, he has had a strong and close association with the sea and seagoing ships. During the First World War, he was a line officer aboard Navy four-stacker destroyers. At one time he served as executive officer and navigator aboard the U.S.S. *McFarland,* flagship of a division of destroyers homeward bound after a tour in the Mediterranean.

There is a lot of open ocean between Naples, Italy and New York City, and Lieutenant de Rochemont was making and rechecking his careful sightings—"shooting" the sun at noon and the stars at dusk and dawn. He was, needless to say, delighted when his logarithmic computations proved accurate and the convoy arrived at New York's harbor on the minute. He could then put away a nagging nightmare—himself standing on the bridge as his ship made her way up Broadway to 42nd Street while he was unable to get her over to the pier!

That was some years ago. Recently it was easier and more enjoyable to double-check the computations and bearings of the mates aboard the S.S. *Christian Radich,* and this windjammer

voyage seemed to offer other pleasures to Mr. de Rochemont's keen eye. One of these may have been watching the young members of the crew get started on a career in the merchant marine—face to face with the elements, for at about the same age Louis de Rochemont began his life with the movies by building and operating his own camera, and then going on to directing, editing and finally producing films.

He has a reputation for turning up new and fresh talent, and for starting new trends. Lauren Bacall, Charles Coburn and Dorothy McGuire portrayed roles before his camera and then achieved stardom in Hollywood. Karl Malden *(Boomerang),* Mel Ferrer *(Lost Boundaries)* and Ernest Borgnine *(The Whistle at Eaton Falls)*— all actors with good stage experience—were introduced to movie audiences through the films of Louis de Rochemont. And while he was a producer with 20th Century Fox, he started the movement to "location shooting" (with *House on 92nd Street),* thereby adding to the reality of the movies. Thus accustomed to taking on new projects and unknown quantities, it is not surprising that he would strive to realize on the new Cinemiracle screen the adventure-filled voyage that is WINDJAMMER.

For all the hard work and problems encountered in such a production, Louis de Rochemont enjoyed his task. At times he dropped his role as producer and undertook the job of ship-chandler for his square-rigger. After the voyage was over he wrote to "his boys" that seeing them and their ship in the Cinemiracle screening room was like never having parted: "... Every morning we meet the *Pamir* together, and in the afternoon Sven Erik and the Boston Pops recall the scenes in Norway that you know so well and I have come to love. . . . It's been a wonderful voyage."

Production Crew

LOUIS de ROCHEMONT III. Son of the producer of *Windjammer*, born in New York City in 1930, educated in various schools across the country, Louis received a liberal arts degree at Dartmouth. While the family was in Hollywood he showed little interest in motion pictures as a career but after the de Rochemonts returned to their home in New Hampshire, Louis started to work on short films during summer vacations. In 1951 he worked on *Walk East on Beacon*. After graduating from college, he handled many different jobs on all sorts of films, from 16 mm through Todd A-O to Cinerama. As everyone else who worked on the Cinemiracle tests, he was excited by the new process. Working with his father aboard the *S. S. Christian Radich,* first as associate producer and later, following Bill Colleran, as director of over 75% of *Windjammer,* he was responsible for developing on film the story of the boys as they came of age during the voyage.

GAYNE RESCHER, A.S.C. One of the most talented young cameramen, Gayne Rescher followed Joseph Brun as director of cinematography on *Windjammer*. He has worked on most of the new motion-picture processes, including Cinemascope, Vistavision, 3-D, Todd A-O, Cinerama and now, Cinemiracle. He was nominated for the 1958 Academy Award for Cinematography (with Harry Squire) for his work on *Seven Wonders of the World,* and his short for Columbia Pictures, *Wonders of Washington,* was nominated for the Oscar as the "best short subject." He attended M.I.T., where he studied aeronautical engineering and was a fighter pilot in World War II. Mr. Rescher's association with Louis de Rochemont began as camera operator on *Cinerama Holiday* and director of photography for the aerial sequence over the Alps in the same film.

COLEMAN T. CONROY, JR. Mr. Conroy began his career as instructor of cinematography in Texas and Louisiana, later he moved to Bell & Howell's professional camera department. In 1952, he joined the Cinerama camera department to work on the first three Cinerama productions. As photographic director of the Cinemiracle camera department, he guided the entire construction and conducted the tests of the first Cinemiracle cameras. Mr. Conroy was the operator of the Cinemiracle camera throughout the shooting of *Windjammer*. His enthusiasm for the wide-screen medium, for close dialogue scenes and for thrilling experiences is great. He did not hesitate to become a "frogman" and undertake the hazardous job of submerging while hanging onto the outside of a submarine.

RICHARD J. PIETSCHMANN, JR. Director of sound for Cinemiracle Productions and *Windjammer,* he served in the Air Force Technical Training Command as electronic instructor. After leaving the service, he became sound engineer for the RCA Motion Picture Division. Later, at 20th Century-Fox, he was assistant chief sound engineer for Movietone News. In 1951 he joined the Cinerama organization and served as director of sound on the first three Cinerama productions. Mr. Pietschmann's experience not only in engineering the Cinemiracle stereophonic sound system but also in the recording and use of high-fidelity sound with this wide-screen process is unique.

MICHAEL MAHONY. Camera technician during the *Windjammer* cruise, he was brought up in the construction business, following in his father's footsteps. He entered the motion-picture industry in 1946 as a "grip," the field in which he could apply his construction talents best. Setting up the weighty Cinemiracle camera in the most impossible places was never a problem to him. No novice at travel, he has also been to most of the out-of-the-way places in the world for Cinerama and *Windjammer*.

JOHN J. WINGERTER. General Business Manager during location shooting of *Windjammer,* he traveled around the world setting up his office ashore or afloat, wherever he could find space. He was first associated with Louis de Rochemont in 1935 on the *March of Time* series, then moved to Time Inc. In 1947 he rejoined de Rochemont during the formation of Louis de Rochemont Associates. During World War II he served with the U. S. Army's Psychological Warfare Branch at Allied Forces H.Q. in North Africa and Italy. He is a graduate of Notre Dame University.

The cast

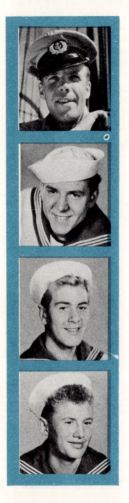

LASSE KOLSTAD, A.B. Lasse Kolstad is one of Norway's outstanding actors and an accomplished sailor. He has played leading roles in such plays as *Our Town*, *The Rainmaker* and singing roles in *Showboat* and *Annie Get Your Gun*. Kolstad is best known to American moviegoers for his role in *The Skating King*. He shipped as an A.B. on the *Christian Radich*, doing all the work necessary as a regular member of the crew. He married Bab Christensen, one of Norway's top theatrical stars while the *Christian Radich* was in U.S. waters.

CADET HARALD TUSBERG. A twenty-two-year-old ex-sergeant, Tusberg has worked in dramatic groups ever since his student days. In 1952 he was granted a scholarship to study in California and, upon his return to his native city of Bergen, was appointed chief of revues for all the junior colleges in that city. He has also worked in Norwegian radio. A competent writer and artist, Tusberg published a ship's newspaper throughout the *Christian Radich's* voyage for *Windjammer* and was often seen sketching the various ports of call.

CADET KAARE TERLAND. After graduation from high school, Terland shipped on the windjammer *Soerlandet*, a Norwegian school-ship bound for Denmark. It was during this cruise that he heard of the *Christian Radich's* forthcoming voyage for Cinemiracle. He had no idea, when he first walked up the *Christian Radich's* gangplank, that he would soon be playing a major role in a motion picture. His blonde, photogenic good looks soon singled him out, however, and he is now a veteran in front of the camera. His ambition is to study radio and television in the United States.

CADET JON REISTAD. Jon will be remembered by *Windjammer* audiences as the cadet who literally dances his collar off in the jump-up dance photographed on the Trinidad dock. Jon is seventeen, the eldest of four boys. His family owns a 2,000-year-old ranch in Eastern Norway. Mounded Viking graves at least 1,000 years old are scattered over the property, indicating that chieftains or kings are buried there. An outstanding sportsman, Jon is also greatly interested in music and dancing. He hopes to win a scholarship to study agriculture in the United States.

CADET FRODE RINGHEIM. Eighteen-year-old Frode was born in the village of Vossevangen in the District of Voss—the birthplace of the immortal Knute Rockne of Notre Dame. During World War II the village was destroyed by German bombing but it is now entirely rebuilt. Like most Norwegian boys, Frode always dreamed of going to sea one day, and his big opportunity came with the Cinemiracle voyage of the *Christian Radich*. On the completion of the voyage, he returned to secondary school and is continuing his education.

CADET PER JOHNSEN. A native of Oslo, twenty-one-year-old Per acted in children's plays from the time he was eight. Both he and Sven Erik Libaek, his boyhood schoolmate and fellow cadet on the *Christian Radich*, appeared in the prizewinning 16 mm Norwegian film, *Tyrihans*, a picture widely distributed in America. A versatile young man indeed, Per plays the drums, shipped as a galley boy some years ago and, in 1955, won the Oslo championship in slalom.

Sven Erik Libaek

THERE are many ways in which an aspiring concert pianist achieves his goal, but I venture to say that signing up for a cruise on a windjammer is not usually one of them.

When word went out that the American film producer, Louis de Rochemont, was in Oslo arranging for the cruise of the *Christian Radich* and selecting a crew, my inborn love for the sea automatically drove me to submit an application. But while I awaited the results, I was torn by all sorts of conflicting emotions. I was eighteen, and my whole life until then was a preparation for a concert career. I had just been awarded a concert date with the Norwegian Philharmonic Orchestra. How could I walk out on something so important? The decision was made for me when I received word that I had been accepted. My parents gave their consent, providing a piano be taken aboard and I practice regularly throughout the voyage. So, when we sailed from Oslo, we took with us an old upright, chained to the bulkhead to secure it against rough weather.

The piano had seen better days, but it gave all of us some very real pleasure during the long stretches between ports. And I kept my promise to my parents, practicing every moment I had off duty. Often, my chair and I would have to be lashed to the deck to prevent us from sliding with the roll of the ship. I had to learn to handle ropes in a special way so that my fingers would not stiffen or my hands become roughened with callouses.

I discovered that several of the boys had had musical training and we organized an orchestra, staging concerts and vaudeville shows throughout the voyage. Our best and most entertaining source material was the native music we picked up at our various ports of call.

When we were cruising in the Caribbean, I wrote to Arthur Fiedler, conductor of the Boston Pops Orchestra, asking him for an audition when the *Christian Radich* reached Portsmouth, New Hampshire. He generously granted my request, and the greatest moment of the whole voyage, for me, at any rate, was that dockside concert.

My decision to apply for the cruise had been a lucky one. How else would I ever have had the opportunity to play the piano with this great orchestra? As a final preparation for the concert, I took a series of coaching lessons with the brilliant Brazilian pianist, Bernardo Segal, while the ship was in New York.

The orchestra was set up on the dock and I took my seat at the concert grand. Arthur Fiedler raised his baton, and the wonderful opening chords of Grieg's Piano Concerto in A Minor flowed over me like the sound of home. My doubts and fears vanished, for I was living this great music. And, after the concert, the warm handshake and approving smile of Arthur Fiedler were heartwarming compensation for the hours of practice aboard the *Radich*. That the Cinemiracle camera recorded all this further heightened the magic of the moment.

The great variety of musicians I met during the filming of *Windjammer*—from natives playing on crude instruments to artists like Casals and Fiedler—convinced me that my life's work had to be music.

Now I await the answer to another application —for a scholarship to study music in the United States. Aboard the *Christian Radich,* my dreams started to come true.

Pablo Casals

Arthur Fiedler

Morton Gould

Windjammer Music

THE MUSICAL SCORE for *Windjammer* was written by gifted, internationally-known composer Morton Gould. His many works, ranging from symphonies to music for the films, include *Fall River Legend,* a Ballet Suite, *Cinerama Holiday, Lincoln Legend,* which was first performed by Arturo Toscanini and the N.B.C. Symphony, and music for Agnes de Mille's ballet, *Rib of Eve,* which had its première at the Metropolitan Opera House.

Morton Gould's score for *Windjammer* is played in the film by the Cinemiracle Symphony Orchestra, conducted by Jack Shaindlin. Mr. Shaindlin has had a long and successful association with both Morton Gould and Louis de Rochemont. For a number of years he was musical director for *March of Time* and is now Eastern musical director for 20th Century-Fox Films. Born in Russia in 1909, Mr. Shaindlin came to the U.S. at the age of fourteen and, a year later, was playing the piano in a silent-film house in Chicago. By the time he was twenty-three he was engaged as a composer for Universal Pictures. He has lectured on movie music, conducted the Ford Foundation TV Program and written the score for many movies. His prolific output for the movies includes MGM's *Teresa,* Louis de Rochemont's *Lost Boundaries* and *Walk East on Beacon* for Columbia Pictures.

Terry Gilkyson and the Easy Riders, who answer to the names of Richard Dehr and Frank Miller, have composed eight songs for this film: the delightful *Kari Waits for Me,* a runaway hit, *The Sea Is Green, Everybody Loves Saturday Night, The Village of New York,* two Calypso numbers, *Sweet Sugar Cane* and *Don't Hurry-Worry Me,* a steel-band version of *Marianne* (a 1957 hit tune by Terry Gilkyson), and a new arrangement of *Life on the Ocean Wave.*

The major musical problem confronting the de Rochemont production crew in Madeira was making a selection from the wealth of material that was available. They finally photographed and recorded performances by the Mountain Shepherds Band and Dancers, the Camacha Dancers of Madeira, and the Folkloric Dancers accompanied by the Hotel Savoy Orchestra. The result is a rich mixture of the primitive with the beautiful, and a feast for the eye and the ear.

There is very little we can add here about the greatest living cellist in the world today that isn't already known. Through the gracious kindness of Governor and Mrs. Luis Muñoz-Marin, the entire complement of the *Christian Radich* was invited to hear a concert by Pablo Casals in the courtyard of the Governor's palace. He was accompanied in a Schubert trio by violinist Alexander Schneider and pianist Mieczyslaw

Jack Shaindlin

WINDJAMMER music is available on a Columbia Long Playing album.

Morton Gould's original score is also available on a Columbia Extended Play recording.

Wilbur de Paris

Richard Dehr

Frank Miller

Terry Gilkyson

Horszowski. The hauntingly beautiful Catalonian ballad, *Song of the Birds,* was played as a solo by Casals, accompanied on the piano by Horszowski. Catalonia, the region in Spain where Casals was born in 1876, has a deep and personal significance for the master cellist. After the Spanish Civil War, Casals went into self-imposed exile and did not emerge from his seclusion until he was invited to perform as soloist and conductor at the Prades Festival. This he did because of his conviction that the music of Bach is the highest manifestation of the human spirit. Casals is now a resident of Puerto Rico, his mother's birthplace, and the island, proud of his family link with the Commonwealth, planned a Casals Festival which has now become an annual tradition.

Alexander Schneider is a member of the famed Budapest String Quartet which made its first public appearance at Cornell University in 1930. Since then it has become a concert institution in the United States, Europe, South America and the Far East. He is among the foremost chamber-music artists in the world and is a distinguished authority on Bach's music for strings. A friend and pupil of Casals, Schneider is also the founder and organizer of the Prades Festival.

The pulsating beat of Calypso was captured for Cinemiracle in romantic old Port-of-Spain. There is a popular saying here that all visitors to the island soon get "Trinidad fever," and

Windjammer was no exception. The gay carnival spirit and the exciting Calypso tunes affected production and ship's crews alike, as the viewer will be when the Calypso sequence explodes upon the screen. Although the Calypso numbers were written for the film by Terry Gilkyson and the Easy Riders, native musicians, singers and dancers performed them with a gaiety and spontaneity which appeared to be inspirations of the moment. The native performers include: the Silvertones Steel Band, the Boys' Town Steel Band, Mighty Skipper, accompanied by Mighter Viper, Lord Superior and Al Thomas, the March of Dimes Singing Sextet, the Limbo Dance Group, featuring Henry (Junior) Trim, Peter Rapsey's Ocean Extravaganza Band and the Port-of-Spain Police Brass Band and Mounted Officers.

New Orleans jazz at its best was introduced into the stereo Hi-fi sound tracks of *Windjammer* as a background to the fascinating distortion photography of New York City by famous lensman Weegee. This was recorded at Jimmy Ryan's by Wilbur de Paris' musical group, consisting of Sydney de Paris, Omar Simeon and Lee Blair. Wilbur de Paris and his band perform in a style that is unique in jazz today. In its collective improvisation it resembles King Oliver's Creole Jazz Band, and there are echoes of Afro-Cuban rhythms in their music-making that are timeless. De Paris was born in Indiana, son of a musician from West Virginia. By the time he was six, he was working for his father in one of his Plantation Shows. He organized a small band in the forties, playing at Jimmy Ryan's. He has a devoted cult which has kept him at Jimmy Ryan's for many years.

Grieg's Piano Concerto in A Minor is played by the Boston Pops Orchestra, conducted by Arthur Fiedler, with Cadet Sven Erik Libaek as soloist. Mr. Fiedler has conducted the Boston Pops Orchestra for twenty-eight seasons, and in July of 1954 Governor Herter of Massachusetts celebrated the twenty-fifth anniversary of the concerts by dedicating the Arthur Fiedler Bridge over the Charles River leading to the embankment where the concerts are held.

As a conclusion, it is to the magnificent strains of the Grieg Piano Concerto that the Cinemiracle cameras take the world's audiences on a tour of Norway's majestic scenes—mountains, valleys, rivers, streams and fjords. It is a tour of breathtaking beauty, and the magic of Cinemiracle does full justice to the grandeur of the country and the music.

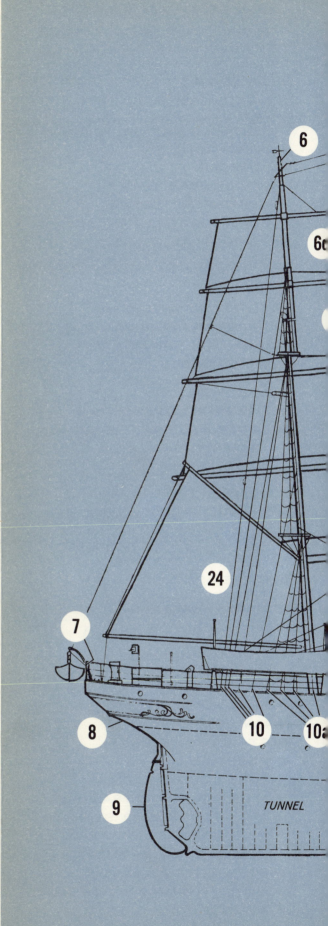

NAMES OF THE PRINCIPAL PARTS OF A WINDJAMMER

1 JIB BOOM
2 MARTINGALE & DOLPHIN STRIKER
3 BOW

4 FOREMAST
4a FORESAIL
4b LOWER FORETOPSAIL
4c UPPER FORETOPSAIL
4d FORE-TOP-GALLANT SAIL
4e FORE-ROYAL

5 MAINMAST
5a MAINSAIL
5b LOWER MAIN TOPSAIL
5c UPPER MAIN TOPSAIL
5d MAIN-TOP-GALLANT SAIL
5e MAIN ROYAL

6 MIZZENMAST
6a LOWER MIZZEN TOPSAIL
6b UPPER MIZZEN TOPSAIL
6c MIZZEN TOP-GALLANT SAIL
6d MIZZEN ROYAL

7 TAFFRAIL
8 STERN
9 RUDDER

10 MIZZEN BACKSTAYS
10a MIZZEN SHROUDS

11 MAIN BACKSTAYS
11a MAIN SHROUDS

12 FORE BACKSTAYS
12a FORE SHROUDS

13 FORE ROYAL STAY
14 FLYING JIB
15 STANDING JIB
16 INNER JIB
17 FORE-TOPMAST STAYSAIL
18 MAIN-ROYAL STAYSAIL
19 MAIN-TOPGALLANT STAYSAIL
20 MAIN-TOPMAST-STAYSAIL
21 MIZZEN ROYAL STAYSAIL
22 MIZZEN-TOPGALLANT STAYSAIL
23 MIZZEN-TOPMAST-STAYSAIL
24 SPANKER

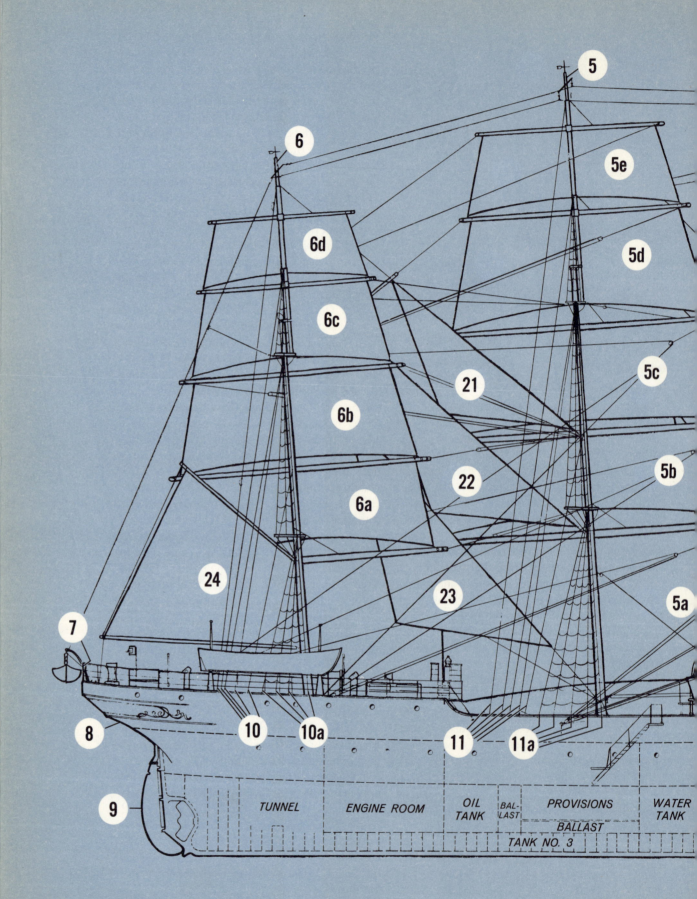

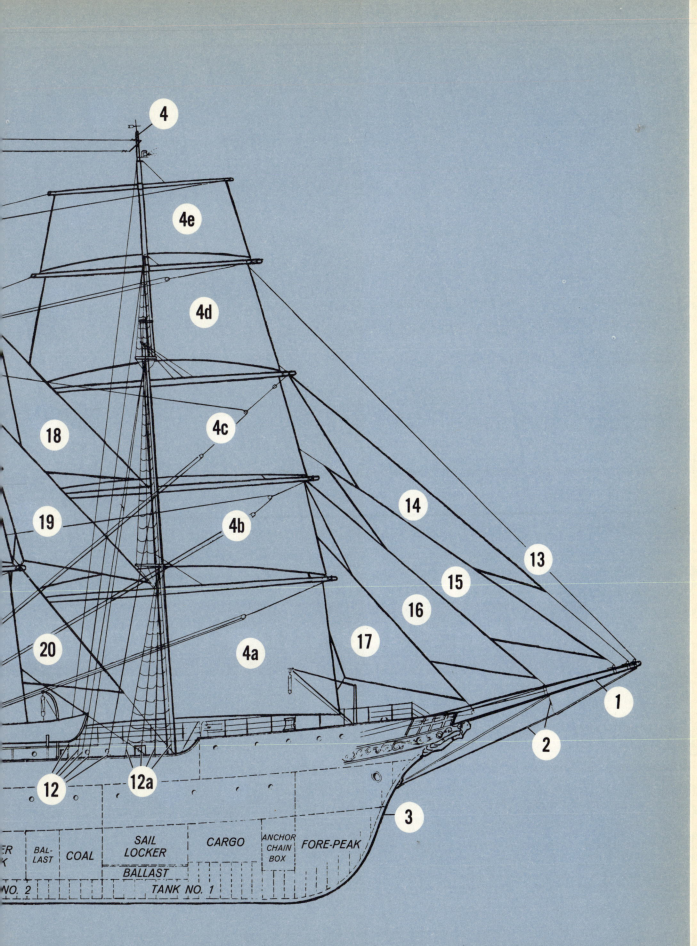

4

4e

4d

18   **4c**

19   **4b**   **14**

13

15

16

20   **4a**   **17**   **1**

2

12   **12a**

3

R	BAL-LAST	COAL	SAIL LOCKER	CARGO	ANCHOR CHAIN BOX	FORE-PEAK

BALLAST

NO. 2   TANK NO. 1

GLOSSARY OF SHIP'S TERMS

 ACCOMMODATION LADDER: A set of steps, going over the side of a ship, down to the water.

AFT: In, or toward the stern.
ALOFT: In the rigging, above the deck.
AMIDSHIPS: In the middle of the ship.

 ANCHOR: An instrument, usually iron, which digs itself into the bottom of the sea bed, holding the ship in one place.

ASTERN: Behind the ship. To go astern, is to move the ship backwards.
AWEATHER: To windward.
BEAM: The width of a ship at its widest point.
BEAT: Tack to windward.
BELAY: Is to secure, or make fast a line.
BILGE: Curve where side of hull meets bottom. Also the nauseous liquids which gather at this point.

 BINNACLE: Housing for the ship's compass.

BITTS: Heavy posts to which lines are made fast. Usually on deck and in pairs. Single post is a bollard.
BLOCK: Wood or metal case for pulleys.
BOATSWAIN: Petty Officer in charge of rigging and deck gear.
BOOM: Spar for extending lower edge of sails.
BOW: The forward end of a ship.
BULKHEAD: Any transverse partition or wall in a ship.

 BULWARK: Solid rail along a ships side.

CAPSTAN: A device for very heavy pulling, usually raising the anchor. Cylindrical ratchet, turned by men using bars, set in capstan like spokes.
COMPANIONWAY: Staircase or steps between decks.

 DAVITS: Derricks on ship's side, used to raise boats from water and swing them inboard.

DECKS: The "floors" of a ship.
FATHOM: A measurement of depth of the sea. Equal to six feet.
FORECASTLE: Raised part of ship, forward in bow. Usually crew quarters.
GALLEY: The ship's kitchen.
GANGWAY: Opening in bulwarks for entering or leaving ship.
HATCH: Opening in deck, surrounded by low wall known as hatch coaming, and supplied with hatch cover.

HAWSE PIPE: Cylinder running from deck above forecastle, out through hull, through which runs the hawse, or anchor chain.

HULL: The body of a ship.
KEEL: A long timber which runs along the very bottom of a ship, from bow to stern.
LEE: The side toward which the wind is blowing.
LINE: A rope.
MAST: A vertical pole for supporting sails and rigging. Named from front of ship to rear, Fore, Main and Mizzen.
POOP: The raised deck at the stern.
PORT: The left side of a ship, facing forward.
QUARTER-DECK: Next lower section of deck, forward of the Poop-Deck.

 RATLINES: Tarred lines set across shrouds to to act as ladder into rigging.

SAILS: Named from the mast which supports them, (fore, main or mizzen) and upwards from deck. First uses name of mast, then follows topsail, topgallants, royal and skysail.
SCUPPER: A hole in bulwark at deck level to allow run off of water
SHROUDS: Heavy lines from mast to ship sides, to support the mast athwartships.
SPAR: Any support for sails or rigging.
STANCHION: An upright post which supports rail or awning.
STARBOARD: The right side of a ship facing forward.
STERN: The whole after end of a ship.
WAIST: Lower part of the deck, between quarterdeck and forecastle.

WHEEL: The steering wheel of a ship.

WINDLASS: A horizontal hand winch for heavy lifting.
YARDS: Horizontal poles on masts which support the sails. The two ends are known as yardarms.

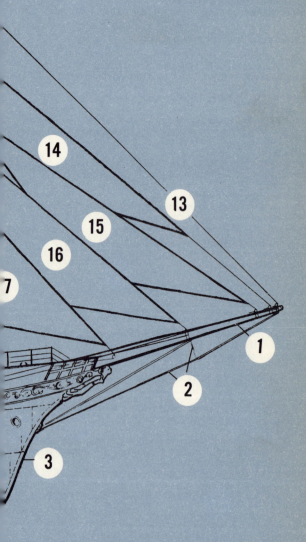

An adventure in color

Our mascot "Stump" doesn't believe in old sailor's superstitions.

"Steady on course southwest by west, sir!"

Liberty for all hands . . . New Year's Eve, Funchal, Madeira.

Carnival spirit in Port-of-Spain.

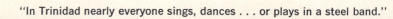

"In Trinidad nearly everyone sings, dances . . . or plays in a steel band."

Caribbean trade winds . . ."Christian Radich" on the port tack.

The Sea Is Green . . . one of nine hit tunes in the repertoire of "The WINDJAMMERS."

"In the Village of New York — they say the buildings grow so tall they push away the sky."

WEEGEE focuses his magic lens o
A fantasy impression of the wor

ork City that has never been seen before.
est city on the world's biggest screen.

"They never dim the lights along the Great White Way; when day is done, the Midnight Sun comes out like in Norway."

Rendezvous on the high seas . . . a fast U. S. Navy Task Force overtakes the "Christian Radich."

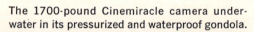

The 1700-pound Cinemiracle camera underwater in its pressurized and waterproof gondola.

". . . Windjammer boys take turns aboard different types of U. S. Navy Ships."

Our Windjammer docks at New York's Battery . . .
a special guest of Father Knickerbocker.

"Come on, girls! . . . Come on, boys! Now's the time to
make some noise—**Everybody loves Saturday Night. . . .**"

Arthur Fiedler conducts our own Sven Erik Libaek and the famous Boston Pops Orchestra in a performance of the Grieg Piano Concerto in A Minor.

"The Grieg Concerto carries us home to Norway . . . and to the scenes each loves best."

Sailing a Square Rigger

by Captain Alan Villiers

IF YOU STAND on the deck of a big sailing ship or look at a model of one in some museum, it looks tremendously complicated. So does the cockpit of a big airplane. Who can get to know all those ropes and their functions in the sailing ship? Who can get to know all those instruments and dials and things in the airplane? The answer is, any intelligent fellow who puts his mind to the job. It may take a few years, yes, for one doesn't learn what is worth learning easily. But there is no dark mystery to either profession.

Let's look at that sailing ship, a full-rigger like the *Radich*. Her crew has to handle her sails, and the officers have to handle the ship. First thing the crewmen must master is to *know the ropes*. Every one of that multitude of wire and cordage ropes has a name, a place, and a function—a belaying pin to be made fast to, a lead in the rigging, a certain job to do which only it can do. There are fixed wires (no ropes) which help support the masts and yards. These are the standing rigging, which stays where it is put, and does not have to be worked. Shrouds, backstays and fore-and-aft stays do this work.

It is the running rigging that matters most to the workaday sailor. The running rigging consists of ropes and tackles that hoist and lower the yards, swing them to get perfect trim to the sails, keep them in position; other ropes pass over the sails themselves, like the gear in a Venetian blind, to pull the sail up and make it possible for the sailors to stow the canvas on the yards.

Think it over for the moment. Sailors could never go aloft and just roll up a great bucking piece of canvas about the size of half a circus tent, with a gale blowing. Such a sail would be quite unmanageable. No, they have to stifle it from the deck first. All the running rigging comes to the deck. That's what helps to make things seem so complicated. Crewmen must know exactly where every single piece of cordage comes from

and what it does. Officers always give traditional orders, comprehended by good seamen right down the ages. When a crewman hears such an order, he must know *instantly* what to do and *exactly* how to do it: what rope or ropes to haul on and how much. His hardest work and his greatest knowledge is called for *on deck,* manipulating the running rigging. Once aloft, it is the strength of his arm and the stoutness of his courage that will finish the job.

Buntlines "bunt" up the sail—pull up, bunt the middle. Clew lines "clew" up the sail—pull up the corners. Leech lines pull in the leech. Braces "brace" the yards—haul them around. Halyards haul up the sails. That's how they got their name—"haul-yards," sailor-pronounced into halyards. Downhauls pull down the sails. Sheets help set them. All these lines take their names from the work they do and are known by the sails they help to operate, like main brace, topsail sheet, topgallant clew lines, and so on. The naming follows a system. The naming of sail, too, follows a system that has evolved through the ages. The "course" is the lowest sail, then comes the topsail (because once it really was the topsail, as in the replica of the *Mayflower* I sailed across the Atlantic the other day), and the topgallant above that and then the royal (like royalty) above the lot. Masts are fore, main and mizzen. Sails add the mast name before their own, becoming foresail, fore topsail, fore topgallantsail, and so on. When ships got bigger, topsails were subdivided. Then you got lower topsails and upper topsails. Sails set on the fore-and-aft stays are jibs if they go to the bowsprit out forward; on any other stays they are called staysails. Like most of the square sails, they are set by hoisting and are taken in by being hauled down. So they have halyards and downhauls too.

Square sails can be set square across the ship, like those of the *Radich's*. Fore-and-aft sails are

Fig. 1: On Starboard Tack

Fig. 2: All Aback

TACKING SHIP

Fig. 3: Mainsail Haul!

Fig. 4: On Port Tack

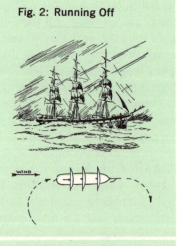

Fig. 1: On Port Tack

Fig. 2: Running Off

WEARING SHIP

Fig. 3: Bracing Yards

Fig. 4: On Starboard Tack

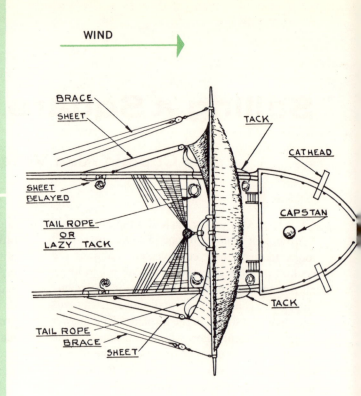

WIND

BRACE
SHEET
TACK
CATHEAD
SHEET
BELAYED
TAIL ROPE
OR
LAZY TACK
CAPSTAN
TAIL ROPE
BRACE
SHEET
TACK

Square sail running free, wind aft

WIND

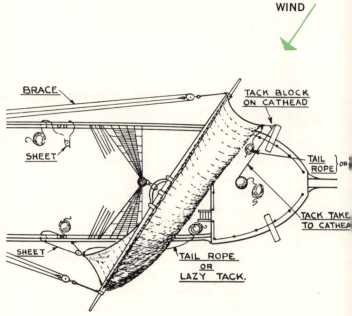

BRACE
SHEET
TACK BLOCK
ON CATHEAD
TAIL
ROPE } OR
TACK TAKE
TO CATHEAD
SHEET
TAIL ROPE
OR
LAZY TACK.

Square sail on a wind, close-hauled

Diagrams used here are by Harold A. Underhill and are from Alan Villiers' WAY OF A SHIP, by permission of the publishers, Messrs. Charles Scribner's Sons, 597 Fifth Avenue, New York City.

similar to those of a yacht. A fore-and-aft rigged ship usually has no yards. She is more simply rigged and can point up to the wind better than a square-rigger. She doesn't run as well and is not so well suited to long ocean passages, and she is not as good a school-ship as a square-rigger because she doesn't make as much work for the boys.

As for ship handling, that is a science that only experience can teach. Briefly, good sailing ships can be made to balance by the set of their sails, and the captain's job is so to operate the power exerted by differing planes of the sails that his ship sets, that he can swing his ship around any way he pleases. On straightforward passage-making, he sets his sails to get the best out of them to provide maximum progress for his ship. He doesn't just hang them up and hope for the best. He has to work at getting the best out of them, all the time, day and night, week in, week out. He has to watch the wind, setting such sails in such a way that the maximum effort is always exerted to bring about forward motion. Unlike the alleged supermen of yesterday, he won't get anywhere by just driving either, for a sailing ship of any design or size will sail at such a rate, and no more, no matter who is driving her. The principal effect of silly driving would be to sail her under, and that has been done more than once, too.

If the wind is against him, he has to *beat,* that is, to tack on a zigzag course, the way a yacht does. Of course, it is a lot harder and much more complicated to tack a square-rigger, but the principal is the same. A boy at a dinghy's helm goes about — puts the dinghy around, on the other tack—by slapping his boat smartly across the eye of the wind, right into wind. So does the square-rigger captain, if the conditions are good. But he has a crew to help him and a vastly more complicated job to perform. He has to alter the trim of every sail in his ship, and he may well have thirty. But he slaps his ship across the eye of the wind, too, so timing his maneuver that his ship swings herself with the planes of her sails, without losing headway. The dinghy helmsman can also *jibe,* if he wants—go around before the wind. So can the square-rigger. That is pretty compli-

cated too, and it takes all hands and the cook to do the job.

To *tack* is to bring the pressure of the wind on the other side of the sails, by putting the ship across the eye of the wind. To *wear* (done by jibing in the dinghy) is to bring the wind on the other side by running off before the wind, and then coming up again with the wind on the other side and the sails retrimmed.

All very simple, isn't it? The airplane pilot, looking at his apparently complicated array of instruments, knows at once what each is telling him. If anything is wrong, he can see it at a glance —and he does something about it immediately. The windjammer captain, looking at his rigging and his sails, takes in at a glance what they have to tell him, too. If anything is wrong, they will shout it to him—and he had better do something about it, immediately! In both cases, that something had better be right. Or else. . . .

All either captain needs is a clear head and perfect knowledge—and a lifetime of experience is a help.

The cinemiracle camera at work

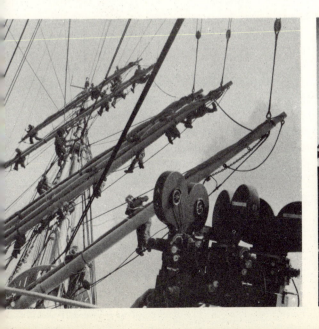

Cinemiracle...

CINEMIRACLE is a new system of photography and projection developed by National Theatres Amusement Company, under the direction of Elmer C. Rhoden, president.

Russell H. McCullough, director of research and development, is responsible for many of Cinemiracle's inventions and has devoted years of research and engineering to the perfection of Cinemiracle.

In 1955, National Theatres acquired worldwide exclusive rights to the Smith-Dieterich patents covering a new and revolutionary electronic camera-lens system developed by the Smith-Dieterich Corporation. This system uses a special three-lens optical system, with a triple 35 mm Mitchell camera, arrangement in which the use of mirrors makes it possible to bring the separate pupils of the lenses into optical coincidence, reducing parallax to a minimum. The center camera records the center picture panel directly through the lens of the camera. The two side cameras, each set at an angle, photograph the right- and left-hand sides of the scene which are reflected in the mirrors. Electrical means are employed to insure the utmost accuracy in image placement during focusing, which is also a development of Smith-Dieterich. The Cinemiracle camera is capable of photographing fast action

what it is, how it achieves its miracles

without distortion through the proper phasing of the camera shutters. It indexes every scene for film threading and sound-recording synchronization. It attains accurate registration with special Dubray-Howell Eastman color film and provides shock-proof protection for each camera lens. Since the beginning of motion pictures, it has been the hope of many engineers to perfect a camera of wide scope without distortion. The Cinemiracle camera photographs a true triple angle of 146 degrees horizontally and 55 degrees vertically—approximately that of human vision.

The camera lens provides a depth of focus from three feet to infinity. Many exceptional under-water shots in Louis de Rochemont's *Windjammer* were exposed with Eastman color negative at F/2.8 with edge-to-edge sharpness. The focus control and the camera motor electrical interlock system are remotely controlled with infinite accuracy. The normal operating speed is 146.25 feet per minute or 26 frames per second. Each frame image is approximately 1 inch wide by 1⅛ inch in height. The camera is quite versatile, without any restrictions, being capable of operating backward or forward with variable speeds. A special view-finder is provided which gives the cameraman a full perspective of any proposed scene.

Cinemiracle's

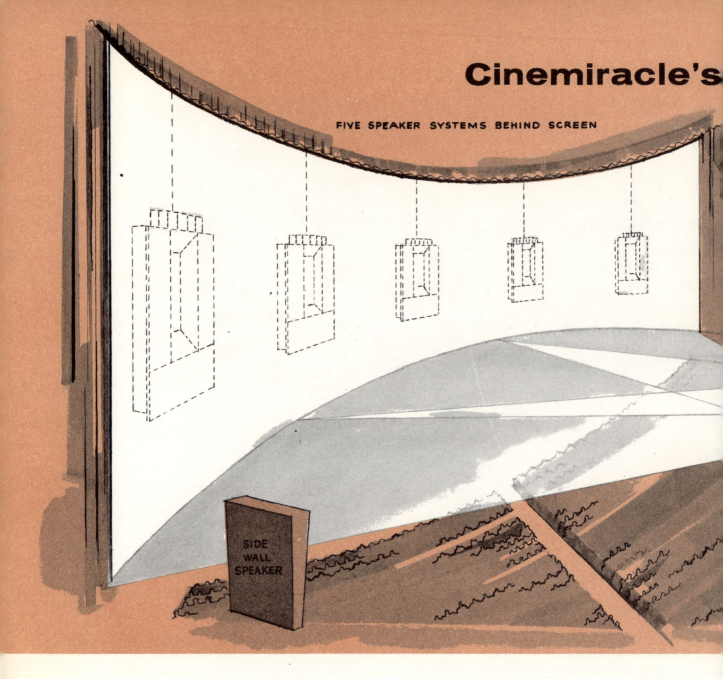

SIDE WALL SPEAKER

Russell H. McCullough, the inventor of Cinemiracle's projection system, started experimental work on this new process over five years ago, prior to the development of the camera, the special printer and other equipment.

Although Cinemiracle is a triple camera and projection system, it is difficult to realize while viewing Cinemiracle's huge curved projection screen that three projectors are actually doing such a precision job. The blending or vignetting of the three projected panels, the perfect registration and steadiness without vibration, the even distribution of screen illumination, the good definition and clarity are responsible for making Cinemiracle a perfected wide-screen process.

In the theatre, three specially designed pro-

jectors are electrically interlocked with a seven-channel sound reproducer in a single compact projection room at the rear of the auditorium. Cinemiracle's projection has a great depth of focus without the blur characteristic of other wide-screen processes. This eliminates eyestrain for the viewers. Cinemiracle projects the picture exactly as it is taken. The viewer sees what the camera sees. Every scene is panoramic as well as a close-up, and every patron lives with the picture. Cinemiracle is most advantageously shown in theatres that can house a screen from wall to wall, but it can be shaped to lesser proportions. The projection optical system, which has been engineered for flexibility, includes mirrors on the two end projectors, and when projected, the

Perfected Projection System

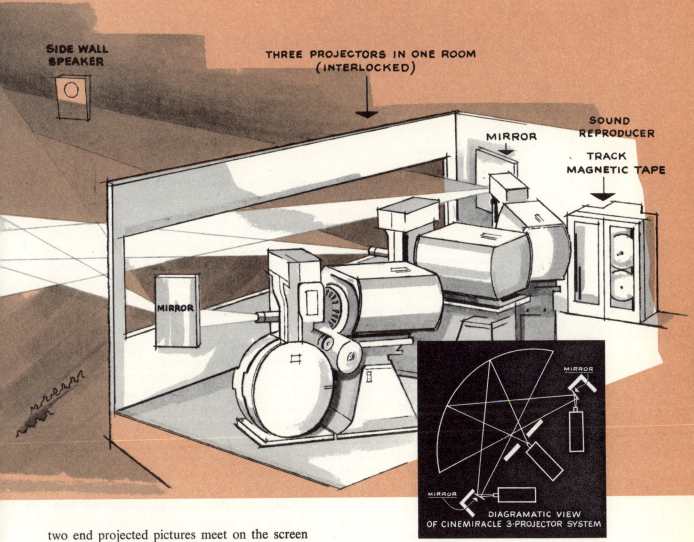

SIDE WALL SPEAKER

THREE PROJECTORS IN ONE ROOM (INTERLOCKED)

MIRROR

SOUND REPRODUCER

TRACK MAGNETIC TAPE

MIRROR

MIRROR

MIRROR

DIAGRAMATIC VIEW OF CINEMIRACLE 3-PROJECTOR SYSTEM

two end projected pictures meet on the screen with the center projected panel, creating one combined elongated picture.

Considerable engineering is responsible for the ease of operation by the projection system and the projectionist. The projection angle must be more or less level with the projection screen, thus eliminating any possibility of elongation of projected objects. The screen's curvature is designed to provide the best viewing angle from all seats without eyestrain. The projectors do not include any mechanical attachments for vignetting the overlap areas. It is accomplished with a specially designed patented printer. It is the first of its kind to be used in any film laboratory. The Cinemiracle printer is provided with film traps, sprockets and guides to hold the film to a very close tolerance for eliminating any possibility of side weave. Each Cinemiracle projector is manned by a highly trained projection technician. After you have viewed the entire Cinemiracle production, more than nine miles of picture film will have traveled through the three electrically interlocked projectors. The speed of each projector is 146.25 feet per minute. Cinemiracle is a giant step forward in motion-picture presentation and its precision is achieved with mirrors.

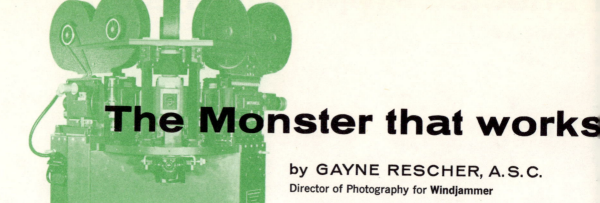

The Monster that works

by GAYNE RESCHER, A.S.C.
Director of Photography for **Windjammer**

SITTING in the theatre, watching the easy succession of scenes in *Windjammer,* it is difficult to imagine the amount of muscle and ingenuity involved in setting the camera and transporting it from one impossible location to another. Fully blimped and ready to shoot, the camera weighs over 500 pounds—a monster of aluminum and wires and optical glass; a maze of electronics and optics, and all for one purpose: to simulate the illusion produced by the human eye.

After a time, we stopped worrying about the physical improbabilities of a location and concentrated on finding the spot where our camera could best tell the story. The problem of transporting and setting the camera was left in the capable hands of our chief grip, Mike Mahony. When he gave me the OK sign, I knew I could go relax or look for the next location and know that when I got back the camera would be in position.

The scene in the tiny radio shack of the *Christian Radich* is a case in point. The door was too small to get the camera through so I told Mike to get it in somehow and left. When I returned, the monster was in. Mike and Kenny Fundus, his partner in crime, had cut away part of the ship to do it! I looked at Mike worriedly, but he simply shrugged his shoulders and glanced toward the ceiling innocently.

Wherever the camera went, it was certain to be followed by our operator, Tom Conroy, and he in turn by our technician, Bob Gaffney. They could often be found in the middle of the night repairing the monster's wounded circuits, or swabbing out its salt-soaked bearings. No mention of Conroy and Gaffney would be complete without acknowledgement of their work in the submarine sequence. They now belong to the very select group that has dived with a submarine while hanging onto the outside!

While photographing the underwater sequence in the coral, there sometimes seemed to be more crew than fish. When we had finished filming this sequence, we all got out of the water, except Conroy and Gaffney who, naturally, were still with the camera. We were just about to signal the winch operator to lift the camera onto the barge when two large sharks darted almost within arms' length. Conroy sensibly enough swung the camera, putting it between himself and Gaffney and the sharks. He claims he was trying to get a close-up but, whatever his intention, it turned out to be an excellent defensive maneuver. The sharks took one look at the monstrous eye and fled.

There are so many more who deserve credit: Fred Montague, our assistant who always timed his arrival with the gelatin filters to coincide with the one wave that would break over the bow; Harvey Genkin, who, instead of mixing oil and gas in advance of refueling the generator, was known to put them in separately and then pick up the entire generator and shake it like a cocktail shaker; Frank Rutledge, my electrician, who vibrated like a tuning fork from the shocks he received while setting the water-soaked arc lamps during the filming of the storm sequence; Salty, Billy, Bobby, Meyerhoff and Dick Falk, who waded ankle deep with me on the salt-soaked deck as our cables carrying 600 amps of electricity became completely submerged; our Norwegian grips, Espenak and Fredriksen, who never learned how to say no.

These are the men who, for me, made the filming of *Windjammer* possible, and this is my way of saying, "Thanks."

miracles ...

Stereo HI FI x 7

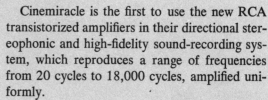

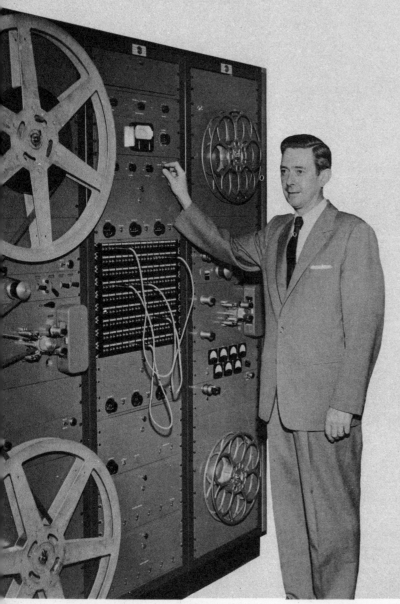

M OST Americans today know high fidelity as an improvement in sound and associate it with radio or phonographs. Actually, high-fidelity sound has been in use in motion-picture theatres for many years. High fidelity is a refinement in amplifier and speaker construction which reproduces the original music without distortion.

Cinemiracle is the first to use the new RCA transistorized amplifiers in their directional stereophonic and high-fidelity sound-recording system, which reproduces a range of frequencies from 20 cycles to 18,000 cycles, amplified uniformly.

When an orchestra is recorded stereophonically, you can notice that different sections play different music scores to make up the complete orchestration or combined frequencies as the composer wished the music to be heard. In other words, while listening to stereophonic directional sound, you will find yourself concentrating on the score played by one or another section of the orchestra.

All Cinemiracle theatre installations include five high-fidelity speakers behind the sound-projection screen and a number of auditorium and side-wall speakers. The seven-channel theatre stereophonic high-fidelity sound system is capable of-reproducing frequencies equal to that of the recording system without distortion.

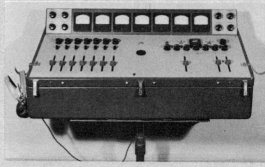

The men behind the machines

RUSSELL H. McCULLOUGH. The man in whose name most Cinemiracle patents were applied for; director of research and development for National Theatres, Inc., and Cinemiracle; member of the National Theatres organization since 1924. Supervised construction of many of the company's finest theatres; responsible for installation of first sound-reproducing system in theatres. A contributor to many technical publications.

P. STANLEY SMITH. Inventor of the Smith-Dieterich electronic-lens system which allows depth of focus at full aperture. Founder and vice-president of Smith-Dieterich Corporation. Has been associated with the Atlas Instrument Corporation as secretary-treasurer in charge of production; with Warner Brothers as Hollywood sound-recording supervisor; and with the RCA Victor Corporation.

GEORGE WILBER MOFFITT. Consultant for the Smith-Dieterich Corporation for the past several years. Formerly astronomer on the staff of the Yerkes Observatory, University of Chicago; optical engineer in the Ordnance Department of the United States Army; research physicist with the Eastman Kodak Company; professor of physics at Washington University, St. Louis. He holds two degrees, Bachelor of Arts, State University of Iowa; Doctor of Philosophy in Physics, Stanford University.

RICHARD C. BABISH. Director of technical film services for Cinemiracle. Formerly laboratory technician for Paramount News, later vice-president and consultant of Vitarama Corporation. With Fred Waller, he was co-inventor of a number of Cinerama patents leased to Vitarama and Cinerama Corporation, an organization which he served for several years as research and development engineer.

Mr. McCullough's staff

Ray Melling
Projection
Research Engineer

Stefan Jan Biskup
Design Engineer

Carl G. Moeller
Design Engineer

Mack G. Lunt
Projection
Research Engineer

Peter Ratkevich, chief film editor, asks the producer to examine one particular section of the more than 678,000 feet of film evaluted for the making of Windjammer.

Here are a few more of the many people who made this picture voyage possible

TECHNICAL ADVISORS
Commander Antoine W. Venne, Jr., USN
Lieutenant Glenn M. Brewer, USN
Alf Bjercke, Oslo
Egil Tresselt, Oslo
Captain Knut Hansen, S/S DANMARK
Captain Paul Heggerstrom,
S/S SORLANDET

ASSISTANT TO DIRECTOR
George Vosburgh

STORY CONSULTANTS
Captain Alan Villiers
James L. Shute

PROLOGUE (35MM) PHOTOGRAPHY
Finn Bergan
Aasmund Revold

SHIP'S SCRIBE
Erik Bye

ASSISTANT FILM EDITORS
Richard Sears
Vito Doino
Jerry Klein

PRODUCTION STAFF
William H. Terry
James A. Petrie
Michael A. Roemer
Ronald Hobin
Ivan Jacobsen
Costa deSala
Jean Pages
Curtis W. Davis

SOUND ENGINEERS
Robert A. Sherwood
James O. Porter
Eugene W. Wood

SOUND EFFECTS EDITOR
Frederick G. White

OSLO

Captain Aksel Molvig, Captain Rudolf Heistand and members of the Eastern Norwegian Schoolship Association
Officers and men of the Royal Norwegian Navy aboard the K.N.M. GARM
The Royal Norwegian Yacht Club

MADEIRA

Staff and Orchestra of the Hotel Savoy
Delegacão de Turismo da Madeira
Dr. Basto Machado
Mr. Vasco Mendes
Mr. Joao Periera
Mrs. Cary Garton
Senhor Toni Nunes

ST. THOMAS

Blue Manta Underwater Swimming Club
Dr. Dean Clyde, leader

TRINIDAD

Boys Town Steel Band
Silvertones Steel Band
Peter Rapsey's Ocean Extravaganza Group
The Honorable Louis Rotant
Mayor of Port-of-Spain
Mr. Mathias J. Oeren
Royal Norwegian Consul in Port-of-Spain

CURACAO

Folk Dance Group of the Peter Stuyvesant School featuring:
Marian Tulleners
Goutje Kanbier
Pastor Siem, Norwegian Seamen's Home
Mr. P. J. Evertsz
Mr. James Leander

COPENHAGEN

Tivoli Gardens
Mr. Henning Soage
Mrs. Inge Bock
Tivoli Boys Royal Guard and Band
Capt. O. E. Qvist, director
Mr. Jorn Tunbo

PERSONNEL AND SHIPS
OF THE UNITED STATES NAVY:

Rear Admiral Joseph C. Daniels, USN
Commander Destroyer Force
Atlantic Fleet

Submarine Squadron Twelve
Capt. W. F. Schlech, Jr., USN, Commanding
Cdr. A. F. Betzel, USN

Underwater Swimmers School, Key West
Lt. Cdr. J. C. Roe, USN, Commanding
Lt. jg. H. A. Jones, USN
J. R. Hazelwood, USN
R. W. Shouse, USN

Officers and Men of—
U.S.S. ODAX (SS 484)
Lt. Cdr. E. Barrett, USN, Commanding

U.S.S. THORNBACK (SS 418)
Lt. Cdr. O. J. Bryant, USN, Commanding

U.S.S. CHIVO (SS 341)
Lt. Cdr. W. D. Dietricksen, USN, Com'd'g

U.S.S. BUSHNELL (AS 15)
Capt. J. B. Hess, USN, Commanding

Commander Russell Crenshaw, USN
Commanding Officer of the
U.S.S. FORREST SHERMAN (DD 931)

Underwater Demolition Team Twenty-one
Cdr. Frank B. Kaine, USN, Commanding
William O'Brien, USN
George Ball, USN

Officers and Men of—
U.S.S. WILLIS A. LEE (DL 4)
U.S.S. MANLEY (DD 940)
U.S.S. GYATT (DDG 712)
U.S.S. STRIBLING (DD 867)
U.S.S. BECUNA (SS 426)

and

Operation "SPRINGBOARD" Task Force 81.3
headed by: U.S.S. VALLEY FORGE (CVS 45)

Orchard   Wingerter   Maloney   Mace   Wolff   de Rochemont III

Louis de Rochemont Associates

LOUIS DE ROCHEMONT has set a pace for his associates that would tax the physical stamina of a strong, younger man, but in doing so he has developed an organization of energetic and alert executives who can point with pride to a list of successful accomplishments.

The word "Associates" in the de Rochemont organization designates the behind-the-scenes co-ordinators; in short, the "doers." These are the men who supervise the various activities of film production that make it possible to meet the "D" (delivery) dates for Louis de Rochemont's pictures. Each man is a graduate of the de Rochemont training school, which means he had become highly proficient in his job before he acquired his title.

Tom Orchard, Lothar Wolff and John Wingerter have been associated with their boss for over twenty years, Orchard as a writer, director and producer; Wolff as film editor, music author-

ity and producer; Wingerter in business and management.

Borden Mace, who serves as de Rochemont's chief executive, is co-ordinator of activity from conception of idea to completion of the product, and Martin Maloney, treasurer, is responsible for business and production co-ordination from budget to financial statement. These men, together with Louis de Rochemont III, the director of *Windjammer,* are the men who guide the corporate ship. Their geographical range of activity —from Rangoon to Djakarta and from Paris to Portsmouth—is complemented by a variety of film activity, from commercial and television production to non-theatrical and theatrical distribution.

"Windjammer" might well be applied to de Rochemont's company because his cadets of yesterday are his chief officers of today, and Louis de Rochemont is the Captain.

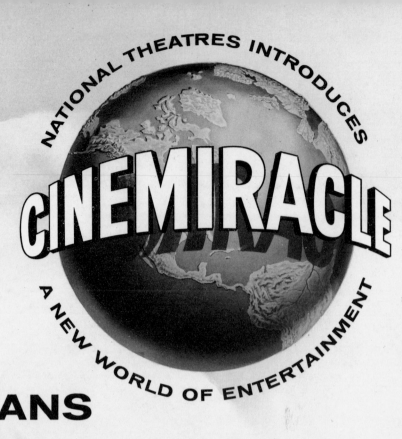

NATIONAL THEATRES INTRODUCES

Cinemiracle

A NEW WORLD OF ENTERTAINMENT

FUTURE PLANS

FIRST AMONG Elmer C. Rhoden's future plans for Cinemiracle is the conversion of theatres in major cities throughout the world. This prodigious task and colossal investment means that projectors, screens, sound systems and other intricate equipment must be manufactured and despatched. Theatres must be converted or new ones built to accommodate Cinemiracle. As the film medium of the space age, a Cinemiracle production can never be shown on the midget screens of the nation's TV sets. Therefore, theatres that are built or converted for this new technique are safe investments and the motion-picture industry's most positive answer to home entertainment.

Film producer Louis de Rochemont, who made *Windjammer* for National Theatres, is under contract for four more features in the Cinemiracle technique. His staff is now working on a shooting script for his next Cinemiracle production.

It was Warner Brothers who first gave the movies the stamp of adulthood by pioneering sound for motion pictures with their film *The Jazz Singer*. Once again Warner Brothers takes the lead in the advance of motion pictures. Elmer C. Rhoden has concluded a multi-million dollar production deal with Jack L. Warner, President of Warner Brothers Pictures, under which that company will produce three spectaculars in Cinemiracle for National Theatres. Warner's first in this new technique is a screen adaptation of Max Reinhardt's famous stage spectacle, *The Miracle*. This has been on the shooting schedule of Warner for several years, but it was not until the advent of Cinemiracle, with its realistic audience participation, that Jack Warner was prepared to go ahead. The picture will be shot on location in Spain with Irving Rapper, director of *Marjorie Morningstar,* handling the directorial reins. It will be the next important production in Cinemiracle to thrill the audiences of the world.

During a recent trip to England, Elmer Rhoden held a series of meetings with British producer J. Arthur Rank. The result was that the Rank Organization will collaborate in the exhibition in England of Cinemiracle with National Theatres.

These are but a part of the future plans of the Cinemiracle organization. Ambitious and positive, but above all, in tune with our times and the desire of audiences everywhere for new and more realistic entertainment. The future belongs to creative man, and with Cinemiracle the future of motion pictures has already arrived.

We hope

you enjoyed

your voyage in

Cinemiracle

Lift this page . . . see the full scope of CINEMIRACLE ❯